AF752252

SONORAN DESERT BESTIARY

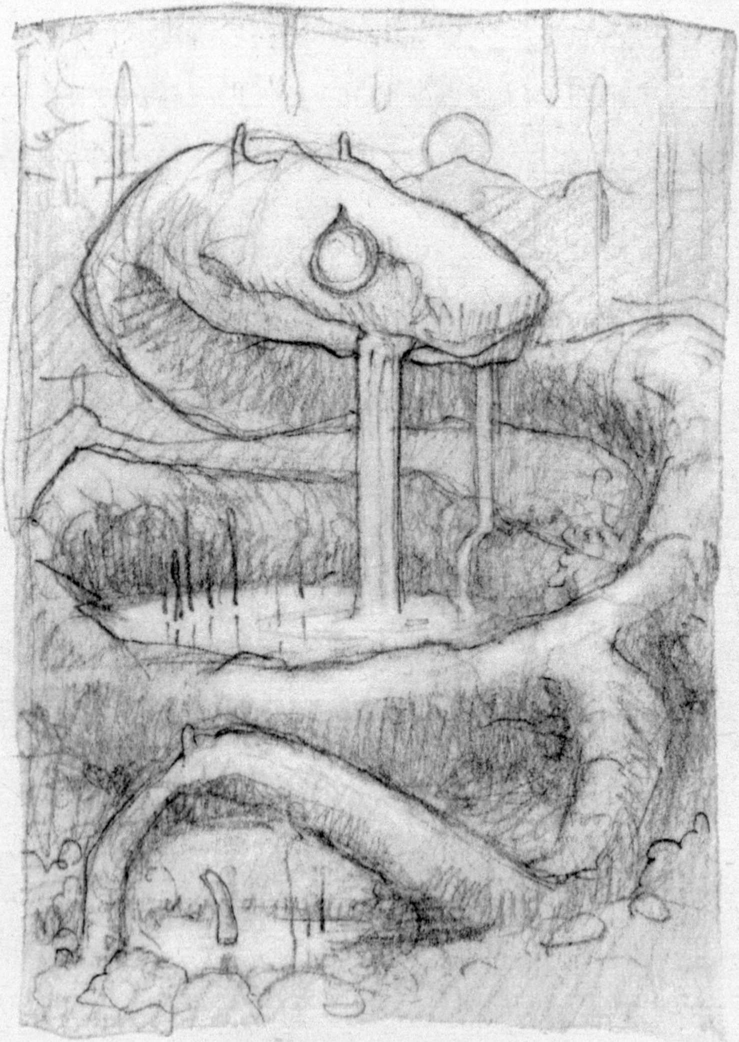

PRAISE FOR *SONORAN DESERT BESTIARY*

"*Sonoran Desert Bestiary* is a delightful amalgam of the material and the imaginal, inviting us to see the desert as a charmed landscape vibrant with creative tensions and deep ancestral wisdom."
—FLORENCE WILLIAMS, author of *The Nature Fix: Why Nature Makes Us Happier, Healthier, and More Creative*

"Be they rumored or confirmed, mythic or cryptic, venomous or hallucinogenic, seldom-seen or ever-present, the creatures described herein are each imbued with nothing short of magic. A book to cherish."
—FRANCISCO CANTÚ, author of *The Line Becomes a River*

"Folklore and natural history collide with delightful results. At turns whimsical, poignant, and haunting, *Sonoran Desert Bestiary* reminds us that the desert is big enough to contain almost anything, and the stories we tell about what might dwell there also illuminate ourselves."
—MELISSA L. SEVIGNY, author of *Brave the Wild River: The Untold Story of Two Women Who Mapped the Botany of the Grand Canyon*

"The ingenious proposition at the heart of this wonderful book is that our fellow beings in the natural world are as strange as our wildest imaginings, while our wildest imaginings—our deepest collective fears and fantasies—produce folkloric beings that are culturally and psychologically real. *Sonoran Desert Bestiary* is an informative, playful, enthralling reminder of how the nature of the land and the nature or our imaginations remain intimately intertwined."
—MICHAEL P. BRANCH, author of *On the Trail of the Jackalope: How a Legend Captured the World's Imagination and Helped Us Cure Cancer*

"A captivating tribute to the Sonoran Desert's otherworldly fauna."
—MICHELLE NIJHUIS, author of *Beloved Beasts: Fighting for Life in an Age of Extinction*

"Robert Long's illustrations look back at you. These beasts are at once observed and invented, as if they've stepped out of science and into dream. They spark a daring curiosity to follow their tracks, with a field notebook and a flashlight."
—PAUL MIROCHA, artist and illustrator of *Coyote's Wild Home*

"This book is a crucial call to action, revealing the hidden lives of the Sonoran Desert's mythic and not-so-mythic creatures, from the humble yet vital Pinacate beetle to the ancient Triops. It is through these stories—blending deep ecology with Indigenous wisdom—that we discover how to live sustainably, ensuring these species thrive for generations to come. Education is the key!"

—RODRIGO A. MEDELLIN, Instituto de Ecología, UNAM

"In Nabhan's latest walkabout, he stumbles into a bar populated by familiar vertebrates, huge imaginaries, little scary stingers, sacred beings, legendary jokesters, puddle-jumpers, leprous shelled ancients, and luminescent feathered dancers. Dragging his capacious intellectual and spiritual backpack and bedroll, he's back in the desert, in dusty campouts with his beasts and their human compañeros who wisely fear and admire them, their predations and predictions told beside a midnight fire."

—RAYNA GREEN, curator, writer, and folklorist

"Robert Long's scientifically accurate and magically beautiful depictions of Sonoran creatures are a perfect complement to Gary Nabhan's stories of the more-than-natural. His illustrations harken back to the work of early artist-explorers who returned with convincing documentation of the sightings of amazing, sometimes fictitious, creatures that most people would never see. As I kept reading, I felt like the prehistoric three-eyed shrimp *Triassic Triops*, with a third eye enabling me to see so much more than I had seen before."

—ELLEN MCMAHON, College of Fine Arts, University of Arizona

"With help from friends of all walks, crawls, flights, and swims, we learn to see, hear, listen, maybe speak with, and certainly learn from the multitude of more-than-human beings that inhabit the richest desert on the planet—to go much farther in order to get much closer."

—ROBERT ANTHONY VILLA, president of the Tucson Herpetological Society

TEXT BY GARY PAUL NABHAN
ILLUSTRATIONS BY ROBERT J. LONG

SONORAN DESERT BESTIARY

A More-than-Natural History

THE UNIVERSITY OF ARIZONA PRESS
TUCSON

The University of Arizona Press
www.uapress.arizona.edu

We respectfully acknowledge the University of Arizona is on the land and territories of Indigenous peoples. Today, Arizona is home to twenty-two federally recognized tribes, with Tucson being home to the O'odham and the Yaqui. The university strives to build sustainable relationships with sovereign Native Nations and Indigenous communities through education offerings, partnerships, and community service.

ISBN-13: 978-0-8165-5420-1 (paperback)
ISBN-13: 978-0-8165-5421-8 (ebook)

Cover design by Leigh McDonald
Cover art by Robert J. Long
Designed and typeset by Leigh McDonald in Bembo Std 11/15, Carolina, and Tomarik (display)

Library of Congress Cataloging-in-Publication Data
Names: Nabhan, Gary Paul author | Long, Robert J. (Robert James) illustrator
Title: Sonoran desert bestiary : a more-than-natural history / text by Gary Paul Nabhan ; illustrations by Robert J. Long.
Description: Tucson : University of Arizona Press, 2026. | Includes bibliographical references.
Identifiers: LCCN 2026010584 (print) | LCCN 2026010585 (ebook) | ISBN 9780816554201 paperback | ISBN 9780816554218 ebook
Subjects: LCSH: Desert animals—Sonoran Desert | Animals, Mythical—Sonoran Desert | Mythology, Mexican—Sonoran Desert
Classification: LCC QL116 .N47 2026 (print) | LCC QL116 (ebook)
LC record available at https://lccn.loc.gov/2026010584
LC ebook record available at https://lccn.loc.gov/2026010585

Printed in the United States of America
♾ This paper meets the requirements of ANSI/NISO Z39.48-1992 (Permanence of Paper).

Dedicated to the memory of Big Jim Griffith,
a desert folklorist with a heart and a humor of
enormous proportions, and to Amadeo Rea,
ethnozoologist nonpareil.

CONTENTS

INTRODUCTION

> *We are drawn to animals, not just because they are lively and pretty, but because we think and dream through them. And a world without an abundance of kinds is bound to be a different world. A humanity without an abundance of animals is bound to be a different humanity.*
>
> —PETER STEINHART, "DREAMING ELANDS," *Audubon*

You might have thought that we would know by now—after decades of living in the stinkin' hot desert—which animals around us were "biologically real" and which were "imaginary." But now we are even questioning the validity of that dichotomy, having read a couple of books that seem to put that facile dualism to rest.

We have become so unsure of our old presumptions that recently, Bobby and I got together to toss some of our old, worn-out books into the fireplace. Then we read these wild words from the gifted and often daffy journalist, Susan Orleans, from her funny, frustrating, and frantic set of essays simply titled *On Animals*:

> How we interact with animals has preoccupied philosophers, poets, and naturalists for ages. With their parallel but unknowable lives, animals offer us relationships that exist in the realm of science and mystery, distinct from the relationships we have with others of our own species.

But just why does the human imagination so often reach into this realm of seldom-seen beings, which occupy that murky, liminal space between fact and fiction?

Why do many of our friends persist in their pursuits of "mythic animals," ones that may have no scientific name nor genetic sample hidden away in some modern-day Noah's Ark of biotechnological intentions?

Why—with all the animals that have been firmly documented around us—do our dreams and glimpses reach for the improbable ones, the apocryphal hybrids, the monstrous, and the miniaturized?

Why do they so often enter our daytime reveries and dark nightmares even today, as they certainly did when we were "mere" children?

And what are traditional elders trying to remind us of when they spin yarns of fanciful, wondrous, or dreadful beasts that still may be hidden around us or among us? How do their perceptions and oral histories of desert animals either complement or stand in creative tension with the stories that desert scientists tell? And what do we do with the projection that 86 percent of all earthly species remain scientifically undescribed, including 6.5 million terrestrial species?

These are the big, hairy questions we ponder in this little book of sketches and stories. While this particular set of questions may have relevance to cryptic and mythic animals found anywhere on earth, we sense that they are particularly significant in desert landscapes, where many of the lives around us are hidden underground, unusually active at night, or fleetingly accessible to us for just a few days each year, when tumultuous thunderstorms crack the parched world wide open.

Our point is that desert creatures elicit from us emotions, recognitions, and suspicions that can hardly be quelled by petting a Persian house cat or even racing a Chinook or malamute sled dog. They bring out into the open the insuppressible desires, dreads, delights, or delusions we may have about how the wild world works (or how, in this day and age, it does not).

If the pets and work-a-day animals around us are not sufficient to help us express what we most fear, love, or dream in our lives, then we perhaps find ourselves inevitably turning to other, more wild creatures to do so. It is not so much that we are constructing, using, or inventing them as it is that they already exist in our psyche, our collective subconscious, and in our most delicious fantasies.

Maybe it is because our overly domesticated species has impoverished the world by driving so many others to extinction that some primordial portion of our psyches feels a desperate need to restore greater diversity of wild, feathered, finned, and furred beings into our lives. It seems ironic to us that the stories we sporadically use to conjure up or "actualize" those phantom limbs, wings, and fins were once entertained by nearly everyone in some desert cultures. Are they now pejoratively dismissed as "animal fables" or "folk tales" by adults who have become fearful of what springs from their own imaginations? It is as if we actually believe that logical-positivist "rational" reasoning about the material world is all there is to life. So we struggle mightily to suppress any images that challenge that logic. This kind of anthropocentric materialism fails to recognize that it has not been rationality alone but also the unfathomably imaginative human spirit that has propelled most cultures to consider new paradigms, heady visions, and disruptively audacious leaps that have enriched the lives of every person on this planet.

To cut to the chase—we need these desert creatures in our bestiary, whether their presences are explainable or not. To paraphrase Claude Lévi-Strauss, they are not only good to taste and savor, but they are also good to think, dream, and dance with!

The following narratives are of two kinds. The first are meditative essays that involve deep reflection on twelve iconic desert creatures or beings that illustrate the creative tensions between

Western scientific knowledge and traditional (largely Indigenous) knowledge. These parables challenge us to give special attention to where these two ways of knowing diverge or converge, rather than assuming that one is "right" and the other "wrong." Clearly, we cannot always find some kind of easy consilience between two or more ways of seeing the natural world, an easy answer that leaves us with a sweet but superficially satisfying "just so" tale or modern fable.

The second set of shorter "prose poems" vastly expands the number of species we recognize in the *Sonoran Desert Bestiary*, but each addresses a question that focuses on the paradoxical nature of the beast. In this expanded bestiary, there is also a greater emphasis on vertebrates and imaginaries. The longer essays implicitly encourage us to pay attention to the meek, minuscule, and modest species among us that may ultimately be as "legendary" as the charismatic megafauna that television documentaries, children's picture books, posters, and T-shirt art are obsessed with. We remind you that it has always been the little beings that run the world, beyond and within us!

SONORAN DESERT BESTIARY

ONE

PINACATE BEETLES

Little Stinkers and Spiritual Guides

Sometimes we unexpectedly meet "spiritual guides" as we walk down paths in the desert that we have frequented many times before.

Early in the morning, during the summer season of monsoons, I walk with Ruby, our Australian shepherd dog, down dusty trails through a mesquite and prickly pear savanna. It's an austere landscape where many of our neighbors might say nothing much is happening, since sightings of mule deer, white-tailed deer, or javelina are not too common during this season.

But Ruby knows otherwise, and I do too, for each morning we greet at least a half dozen fellow travelers—desert stink beetles, as some of my neighbors call them. These darkling beetles are out doing their walking meditation just as we are, but when Ruby edges near them, they often stand on their heads, striking the *sirsasana* pose that many Americans know as the yoga headstand.

Ambling shard of burnished obsidian
bridges Hades and Heavens.

At that point, Ruby moves away, and I offer each of them a bow and a prayer with my hands folded together, before we continue our way through what one of my friends kiddingly calls the "dry lands where nothing much is supposed to happen." Once Ruby backs off a little, neither my passing nor that of the dog seems to provoke them to do very much more than keep still with their heads in the soil. I ease back into my contemplative trance, and perhaps these pinacate beetles do the same.

Sometimes we barely glimpse the presence of a legendary animal in our midst until something or someone makes it larger than life. Within short order, that very same animal seems to make cameo appearances wherever we go, and we can't get enough of it. Most humans appear not to care for little creepies. Moreover, many urban dwellers miss the crawlies, stingers, and stinkers doing headstands unless a memorable story is put before them. Only then do we begin to watch or listen to them more intently, to offer them our affection, and to feel an affinity between their lives and ours.

If I recall correctly, in late winter of 1983, I strapped my eight-month-old son, Dusty, into an infant backpack carrier and began the steep climb up Pinacate Peak on northwest Mexico's largest volcanic shield. We were accompanied by four old friends, two of whom knew the terrain there very well. Before that climb, I had only vaguely been aware that the peak shared its name with darkling beetles. Perhaps the peak was named for them because its dark silhouette also stands up, high above the desert floor. In a certain light, both could be seen with a brilliant sheen on their otherwise pitch-black exterior.

Their name comes from the Spanish term *pinacate*, derived from *pinacatl* in the Nahuatl tongue. That ancient way of speaking and knowing is best known as the language of the Aztecs of central Mexico. Metaphorically, the term *pinacate* has also come to refer to someone who stays as still as a stone, head down in the ground, rather than poking it upward, aspiring to greater heights.

Over centuries, the use of the Hispanicized Nahuatl term has spread all over Mexico and the desert U.S. Southwest as the most common "handle" or folk name for the tenebrionid beetles in the genus *Eleodes*. My guess is that the sacred peak that local Hia-Ced O'odham families have always called S-cuk Do'ag may have received its name from early Spanish colonizers, simply because of its likeness to the beetle in color and form. Tens of thousands of Mexicans and Americans use the term *pinacate* to this day. Like a cactus thorn, it has stuck, becoming a fixture in Sonoran Desert lore.

To my surprise, when the five of us peaked four hours later on the sacred summit of a thirty-by-forty-mile volcanic shield, our gracious guide, Ray Turner, alerted us to the next saga of our adventure:

> As soon as you all have rested a bit, had water, and dropped your packs, you should get ready to be photographed standing on your heads, just as Godfrey Sykes had urged his colleagues to do here in 1907. Since that time, it has been a tradition that all of those who reach the summit of the Sierra Pinacate must stand on [their] heads just as the pinacate beetles do.

Say whaaat? I had seen many carapaces of dead beetles, and perhaps one or two live ones tipping their carapaces at strange angles, but did they really stand on their heads? Yes, indeed, said Ray, a fine desert ecologist who had climbed Pinacate Peak many times over the four decades before reaching the summit with us that day. Having known the Sykes family for years as neighbors and friends and worked in the same desert lab on Tumamoc Hill, Ray had always tried to honor the fine, upstanding tradition that Godfrey had begun three-quarters of a century before our group's climb to the summit. Since Godfrey Sykes's first ascent of the peak, perhaps dozens, if not hundreds, of desert hikers have taken time to turn their lives upside down as a means to maintain this sacred ritual.

Down on our hands and knees in black volcanic pebbles, we prepared ourselves for the momentary uprising, and when Ray's camera timers were ready to go and ticking, we all hoisted ourselves up on our hands and heads to form tripods for a moment of collective glory.

Dusty crawled around nearby, no doubt wondering what we were doing and why he was missing the fun. And so, when the cameras were readied once again, I stood behind Dusty and held his ankles so that his head would be grounded, and his butt would be up to the creator or whoever else might be looking down on us for that New York minute. As if to concur with our choice of solemn rituals, Dusty delightfully giggled the entire time his diaper was held higher than his head.

On the way back down to our campsite at Suvuk, or S-wegi in O'odham (the place of the red-hued lava flows), I decided to ask Ray the most obvious question of the day: "While I know why we decided to stand on our heads, why do the pinacate beetles stand on theirs?"

Sometimes Ray could be a man of few words, as I learned over forty-five years of friendship. A tall, rugged-looking, handsome man, he would often pause before offering an incredibly lucid answer to any question thrown at him: "Defense," he simply replied as we continued to stumble and tumble our way down through a boulder field of lava cobbles. "Defense?" I questioned, not seeing many assassin bugs, pirate bugs, wolf spiders, daddy longlegs harvesters, or other adversaries out there on the lava shields where the darkling beetles abound. "Speaking of defense," Ray confirmed, "watch your step," he added, "I think I heard a rattler somewhere under the basaltic cobbles just ahead of you."

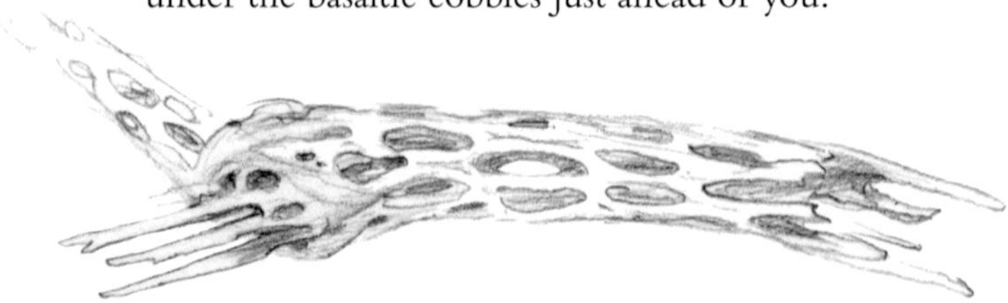

I became so preoccupied with watching my step that I forgot to take up the topic with Ray again when we got back to camp. But every summer after that, I had the great honor of seeing darkling beetles present at some place or another—from Utah and Nevada to Arizona and Sonora. There, the pinacate beetles positioned their posteriors as high as they could go, if only for posterity's sake. I developed a deep affection for them, even though I only climbed their namesake peak two more times to elevate my own butt high above the volcanic cobbles so it could dwell a moment up with patches of perlucidus clouds in the heavens.

Perhaps this eccentric ritual became for me the way I developed my lifelong affinity for darkling beetles. Sometimes the mere act of emulating "the other"—in this case, the darkling—brings us closer to appreciating the distinctiveness of its own charisma. As Oscar Wilde famously quipped, "Imitation is the sincerest form of flattery," and I suspect that darkling beetles unreservedly accept all the flattery they can get.

After the ascent of Pinacate Peak, I gradually came to realize that I should not merely watch the beetle named *Eleodes armata* but should take a whiff of its stinkingness.

Now, darkling beetles are also called stink beetles, and for good reason: they smell terrible when provoked, or even as they expire. When they take a defensive posture by standing on their heads, the darklings are decked with a rather repelling, repugnant, and altogether repulsive scent.

They spray a horrid odor out of their rear, which is to say, from the tips of their lower abdomen. When they are standing on their heads, you might say that they spray it out from the *upper* abdomen, because that is what is closest to the heavens at that moment.

The oily, musty stench they eject can fly ten to twenty inches before it slimes their adversaries. It is dominated by quinones, chemical compounds so potent that they are poisonous at high doses; at low doses, they can function as antimicrobial, antifungal, antimalarial, anti-inflammatory, and anticancer agents. But for all the good they may do in the world, quinones are rather irritating, toxic chemicals that smell a bit like a zombie's wedding bouquet of chlorine, formaldehyde, and noxious darkroom chemicals.

For years, I have watched the pinacate beetles around our second home-of-sorts in the Comcaac fishing village of Desemboque del Sur. But it took me a while to ask any of our Comcaac neighbors about them. When I finally worked up the nerve to query some elders regarding any traditional knowledge they might feel comfortable sharing about pinacate beetles, it was prompted by a provocative passage in the writings of one of the most beloved of all scientists of North American deserts, Edmund Jaeger.

Jaeger worked for decades on desert ecology from a cabin outside Palm Springs, where he was often joined on his camping trips by seven others known as "the Creative Brotherhood." They were awash with interdisciplinary insights about life in arid lands that arise only when field-worthy individuals share ideas around a campfire. In 1950, Jaeger wrote that an unspecified clan of Native Americans whom the Brotherhood had encountered believed that the reason pinacates stood on their heads was "to listen to spirits."

"Holy *mole*!" I thought to myself. What a remarkable insight. But Jaeger did not divulge what Indigenous culture or cultures retained this belief, so I thought it was fitting to ask knowledgeable individuals in the Comcaac community what they thought of this assertion.

On two consecutive days with temperatures reaching above 110 degrees, I walked through the blistering heat to the homes of Manual Monroy and Maria Luisa Astorga to sit in the shade with them and learn what they knew or thought about this belief.

Manual is a rather quiet, thin, no-nonsense guy whom I have known for decades. He lives three blocks inland from what has become our second home for the last two decades, right on the shores of the Sea of Cortés. I often turn to him for a first opinion regarding any issue in desert natural history. When I asked for his opinion about why the beetle he calls *conteetxyat* stands on its head and stinks, his initial answer was cautionary:

"Oh, horny toad, I think I casually told you a story about the pinacate beetle and the coyote about a decade ago, but it seems you were so focused on coyotes as tricksters at that time, you didn't notice that the pinacate was really the focus of the story."

I laughed, feeling a bit silly that I had not paid attention to the pinacate beetle in his story. "Sorry, I missed that part."

He sighed, then waved away my apology, showing that he forgave me for my poor memory and spotty attentiveness.

"Well, let's start over. The pinacates do raise a stink as a form of defense, and I suppose they stand on their heads to spray the stink a bit farther. But why don't I come over to your house at breakfast time tomorrow for coffee, and you can get out your notebook to help you record and remember the entire story about *conteetxyat*."

"That would be good," I said, "So I'll have some coffee ready for you right after sunrise."

As we drank coffee together on my porch the next morning, I confessed that my renewed interest in the story had been prompted by something I had recently read—a passage about pinacates that had been penned nearly three-quarters of a century ago.

"Last week, I read that some Indians in the Mohave Desert in California believe the beetles stick their heads in the ground to listen to spirits," I said.

Manual's eyes sparkled as he chuckled. "Well, that could be, but it's only partially correct. Our people do say they are listening when they stand on their heads, but that is not the whole story. In a way, it is also another means of defense against Coyote."

As he went through his version of the story in more detail, I realized that the pinacate's other form of defense against Coyote could be called "tricking the trickster." When I had finished taking down the entire story, he reminded me that each storyteller in his village has his or her own version of it, so I should talk with others and then come back to him for more discussion.

The next day, I walked two blocks in another direction to ask Maria Luisa Astorga, who was eighty years old at the time, if she knew much of the story of Pinacate and Coyote. She smirked, then nodded. When I asked whether the *conteetxyat* listen to spirits when they place their heads below ground, she laughed out loud. Although Maria Luisa is now bound by a wheelchair or walker, she became very animated and amused once I had asked her my question. She simply replied, "You must know that entire story to understand that. Then you can decide for yourself."

My translation here is a composite of Manual's and Maria Luisa's renditions of Pinacate and Coyote. Following Manual's suggestion, I tried to get as close to the "entire story" as it might be possible for a non-native speaker to do, since some storytellers embellish one part but leave other fragments out of their version. Of course, any translation from the ancient language of Cmique Iitom through Spanish to English inevitably loses something along the way, but here it goes:

Coyote was ambling along a well-worn path when he saw a pinacate beetle—*conteextyat*—standing on his head in the sand next to the trail. Coyote was so hungry that he was about to eat the beetle even though he knew it stunk, but his curiosity got the best of him. Perhaps he might divulge some juicy gossip about their neighbors if he talked to the pinacate before eating him:

"You little acrobat, why are you clowning around, standing upside-down like that?" Coyote asked.

"I'm listening to voices," the *conteextyat* whispered.

"Whaaat?" Coyote queried, still hoping to pry more information out of him before deciding whether to eat him. "What are they saying?"

"Well, it's not good . . . not good for you. They are tired of you stinking up the neighborhood by always pooping right in the middle of the trail. You coyotes can wander anywhere you want, so why do you decide to crap right where the rest of us walk, making the place smell to high heavens? They are tired of it. They say that many are coming to hunt all of you down and kill you. If I were you, I'd flee right away before you lose your life!"

Coyote was scared out of his wits. He immediately responded with alarm, forgetting his interest in eating the pinacate, and loping off to a remote desert mountain range, where he hoped they could not find him and snuff him out. Of course, he never thought of alerting the other coyotes to the plot to kill them; he merely wanted to save his own skin.

And so, Coyote ran and ran until he found a cave-like burrow high on the side of a mountain to employ as his hideout. He was so afraid of being seen and apprehended that he only came out of hiding to poop on the trail immediately in front of the cave, before returning to his hidden haunts.

Not one member of their desert community was bothered by his absence, for none of them were tricked out of any of their possessions since he disappeared. In fact, they were relieved that they no longer had to suffer his antics. But after a while, the pinacate beetle went out on a pilgrimage to see whether Coyote was dead or alive.

It was easy to find him because Coyote was dumb enough to leave a pile of crap in front of his burrow, and the beetle could smell it from a distance. The pinacate beetle hid behind a rock, and after a while, spotted Coyote coming out to quickly defecate. He looked thin and emaciated, a shadow of the braggard he had once been. When Coyote glanced up while doing his duty, he noticed that he was being watched. He growled at the pinacate.

"Why did you tell me that they were all out to get me? Only *you* came after me! You tricked me!" he yelled, bawling out the beetle. And yet he was too weak to attack the *conteextyat*. The pinacate

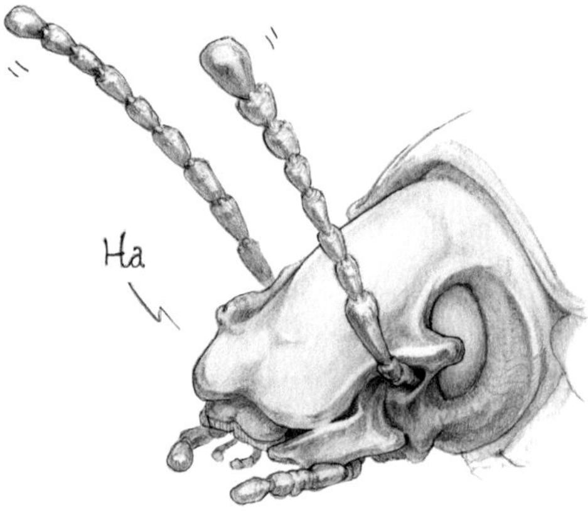

"He and all the others in the neighborhood knew full well who among them had always made his living as a Trickster!"

didn't have to say anything. He and all the others in the neighborhood knew full well who among them had always made his living as a trickster!

We might surmise that the pinacate was not merely stinky, but so witty that he could defend himself from anyone. But even pinacate beetles occasionally get the tables turned on them. Only one of the many rodents that live in the Sonoran and Mohave Deserts has figured out how to overcome *conteextyat*'s obnoxious chemical defense. The little grasshopper mouse sneaks up on a pinacate beetle when it is not looking, deftly grabs it, and jams its lower abdomen deep into the ground so that the *conteextyat* cannot spray it. Then the mouse chomps down on the exposed upper half of the beetle's body, killing it for a meal. The odor of the dying beetle remains stuck in the sand.

There is something endearing about one of the most odiferous creatures of the North American deserts calling out Coyote for leaving his own odors along every trail in this arid region. You may say that it is much like the pot calling the kettle black, but perhaps the pinacate doesn't see it that way. He may be too busy "listening to voices."

When the monsoon season ends, I often find a litter of new pinacate hatchlings hanging around anthills, where some of these infants wander around seeking breakfast. Occasionally, I see one of the little ones practicing the art of standing on its head. By immersing their heads in the ground, they have found a wonderful way to be in touch with the earth itself, attentively listening to whatever wisdom or warning it may offer.

That is why I find it curious that these toddlers are both "little stinkers" with ample defensive tactics *and* "contemplative spiritual guides" at such a young age. They may indeed be "darklings" as their smooth, reflective carapaces rise off the ground, but then they become beacons, for when the light of the dawning sun shines upon them, they reflect their brilliance out into the waking world.

I find it intriguing that Western science and Indigenous knowledge have such distinctive ways of shining their peculiar lights onto the lives of pinacate beetles. Desert ecologists will argue that the beetles gain some selective advantage by raising their hindquarters into the air to spray their noxious scent farther to repel predators. And yet some Indigenous peoples read something else into this inversion: that the beetle humbly lowers its head down to earth to listen deeply.

I am grateful for both views of this inverted posture. When gently juxtaposed in our minds, we might one day find a way to reconcile these two perspectives, rather than assuming one is right and the other wrong. I am richer when I hold both before me.

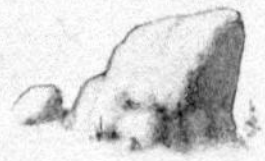

JEJENE SAND FLIES

In Mexico and the desert Southwest, they are called *jejenes,* an old Spanish word for gnats, but gnats they are not. Called sand flies, biting midges, or punkies in English, the sand stretches of the Sonoran Desert shores and dune fields are dominated by *Culicoides sonorensis.* Because they are hardly bigger than the point of a pen—hardly ever reaching a sixth or eighth of an inch in length—they are fondly called *no-see-ums,* for they make true mosquitoes, gnats, and flies look like massive monsters. Douglas Brown has aptly referred to them as the "single most significant animal" of the Mexican beaches along the Pacific because of their enormous capacity to drive you absolutely crazy once the females begin to feed on your blood. Although both sexes of *jejenes* are floral visitors that nourish themselves on pollen and nectar, the females need red blood in their diets for their eggs to develop properly. And so they have found a treasure trove of human skin to drill into from Memorial Day through Labor Day each year when both Mexicans and Yankees go to the beaches of Sonora and Baja California to burn their skin and drink a few Coronas or *micheladas* at sunset. Although they can't be seen, as their tiny scimitar mouthparts cut into human flesh, their victims soon know that they have been bitten, for a painfully irritating sensation is suddenly felt, and is soon followed by a red welt or watery blister. One in four beachgoers may be allergic to the bite. The *Culicoides* sand fleas transmit a bluetongue virus, which is not contagious but can cause swelling in humans and death in sheep, goats, and cattle. I once had the honor of being swarmed by the little suckers in a sandy patch just north of Caborca, Sonora, as I tried to sleep at sunset on a misty summer night. I was so "taken" by the female sand flies that I writhed in my sleeping bag for two hours straight before giving up and locking myself in the cab of my pickup truck with the windows rolled up. Only a bit of *mezcal bacanora* saved me from going insane that night. Can you guess whether it was best employed as a salve on my blistered skin, or drunk as *traegitos* every hour until I fell unconscious and remained so until the first light of dawn, when I beelined it home to nurse my wounds?

TARANTULA HAWK WASPS

Tarantula hawk wasps belong to a family of insects called spider-hunting wasps and often aggregate with other flying insects around milkweed blooms in the summer. I was out by the Canelo Creek cienegas, intent on netting and banding monarch butterflies and their close kin, so I didn't quite notice that a tarantula hawk wasp had hopped into my net with the other pollinators and nectar robbers. As I tried to gingerly remove a monarch from the net, a two-inch *Pepsis grossa* nipped my index finger, and I was suddenly forced to take notice of its presence. The feeling of its sharply curved stinger jabbed a half inch into a rip in my flesh was far more euphoric than my former encounters with bark scorpions, stingrays, and killer bees. As my late great friend of three decades, Justin O. Schmidt, reported, the effects of its sting were "instantaneous, electrifying, and debilitating," so much so that I experienced painful throbbing not only in my finger but in my entire hand. I somehow dumped all the captures in a jar, hopped back into my car, and drove home as fast as I could to ice my entire hand for the next hour. Justin—also known as the "King of Sting"—ranked tarantula hawk envenomization as the most painful in North America, beaten only by a bullet ant from South America, which remains at the apex of agony. Of course, that poison's potency did not evolve to harm humans, but to paralyze their spidery prey to the point that the wasp can drag them home and eat them alive. If we were any more observant—speaking for myself and oodles of tarantulas—we could have escaped harm by noticing the aposematic coloration of its mean orange wings against its shiny black thorax, which is meant to be a clear warning that if we don't like being stung, we should simply get the hell out of the way. Yet little did I know that simply by joining the list of the tarantula hawk's intended victims, I would gain the admiration and jealousy of thousands of young bloods who have become obsessed with experiencing the ecstasy of close encounters with the "top ten" on the world-famous Schmidt Sting Pain Index. One enthusiast came from Kentucky just to be stung—where I had been—in the Sky Islands . . . so close to heaven and so far from a poison control center. Would I do it again, just for the thrill of it, or to merely to elicit the envy of entomologists?

TWO

TRIASSIC TRIOPS

Dinosaurs and Saints of Waiting

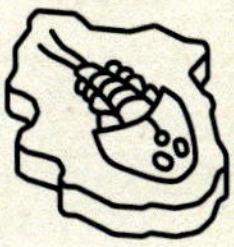

Dinosaur shrimp. Triassic Triops. Three-eyed shield shrimp. Long-tail tadpole shrimp. Seldom-seen shrimp. So many names for one of the most minuscule and cryptic of all mythic creatures!

On top of that, they hardly ever appear when and where you wish to see them. The eggs of these desert shrimp can rest as cysts that resist desiccation, damaging radiation, and damnation for years on end without dying, then hatch out by the millions after a single forceful gully washer. In fact, they outlive many of the field biologists who are fortunate enough to witness them once, then wait years for another mass hatching. The patient and perspicacious field geeks turn old, gray, and in the way before these little dinosaurs deem it worthwhile to break out of diapause again.

Recently, it dawned on me that I hadn't glimpsed a single dinosaur shrimp for decades, and my days were probably numbered.

A third eye orients me in depth-space
but not in time.

I decided it might be time to mount a minor expedition to search for them again. In fact, my last sighting of one was during an earlier millennium, in a side drainage of the Grand Canyon. It was at a curious place in the canyon where white and gray dolomites from the Devonian period were laid down as sediments in a sea. That was curious to me because the lineage of dinosaur shrimp is claimed to be a "living fossil," as they have remained relatively morphologically unchanged for upward of 225 to 250 million years. And yet that living fossil status has recently been challenged by paleontologists, so the shrimp might be forced to give up their AARP and Social Security cards.

I was feeling as if I had not been evolving much either when I confessed to my next-door neighbor, Jack Zittere, that I had a hankering to see a dinosaur shrimp again. The way he stayed silent for a moment hinted to me that it might be hard to do; I guessed it would be a long shot that he could arrange a meeting with one on short order.

To my amazement, Jack—a field ecologist by profession—generously responded in less than a week with a photo of the suspect, and a map of where he had sighted the famed *Triops longicaudatus* less than a ten-minute drive from our neighborhood.

Once my expedition team arrived at our destination, my Aussie shepherd dog hopped out of the vehicle first to sniff around. My wife, Laurie, and I unloaded the trunk full of the jars, magnifying glasses, scoops, and colanders we thought we'd need to make a "catch" and an "identification."

We had assumed we would need to take a long hike down an unpaved road badly damaged by mining exploration before we found anything. But it happened that there was a patch of muddy water right where we parked the car, near a junction with the paved rural highway and the dirt track. The Aussie plunged right into it.

It must have been a rude awakening for the motley crew of *Triops* hunkered down in the shadows of the puddle, because they began to scurry around, each of them with more legs than I could count.

It was probably the very same puddle that Jack had mentioned to us in his text message as a good place to turn off the pavement and park. It wasn't very pretty, and the water was rather murky, so much so that I had to get on my knees to get a closer look at the little dinosaur-like scramblers, who seemed to be surviving well even though it had been several days since the most recent rain. But being knee-high above them was still too distant. I had to go down on all fours to get the perspective I needed, and then, for an even better glimpse, slip down on my belly in the mud.

I remembered then what has been prophesied by so many spiritual leaders from around the world: when we prostrate ourselves and pray for a miracle, we sometimes find the answer to our prayers right before us (on earth).

Once I had humbled myself enough to immerse both my knees and hands in the mud, I got a good look at one miniature dinosaur treading water at one side of the pond. At about the same time, Laurie found another swimming in an eddy on the other side and edged up to it. We had gotten eye to eye—or two eyes from each of us to three eyes from each of them—with one of the tiniest but most widely occurring mythmakers in the world.

That last fact was what tickled me so much as I knelt there with the legendary three-eyed shield shrimp in my little metal cup. In unusually wet years all around the world, it seemed ubiquitous, but with the increasing frequency of extended droughts, it seemed impossible that anything might survive in its favorite haunts.

This diminutive creature—the most mythmaking of all the Triassic *Triops*—persists on at least three continents, some 300 million years after its lineage bet its destiny on ephemeral pools of freshwater and diverged from most other shrimp- and crablike critters. Most of its ancient kin stuck with saltwater. Although they look like miniature horseshoe crabs, they split the evolutionary sheets and went their separate ways long before the first humanoids began to salivate over shrimp sandwiches in crab shacks on the seashores of the world.

Soon we found them in microhabitats other than mud puddles; as we continued up a canyon, we came to a series of connected bedrock-bottomed pools called tinajas, each with a few shrimps in them. They seemed more active in the slowly cascading stream that connected the chain of tinaja water holes descending like a stairway. There was all manner of sedges, wetland grasses, grapevines, and wildflowers edging those pools, with elderberries, wolfberries, and sumac bushes clinging to the rocky slopes along this clear but slightly alkaline flow of fresh water.

After we got over that superficial resemblance to the horseshoe crabs in the ocean, we were touched by their distinctiveness. The three-eyed shield shrimp were not famed because they were rare, for they are not. They became legends for suddenly appearing by the tens of thousands after rains in the oddest of places. They popped

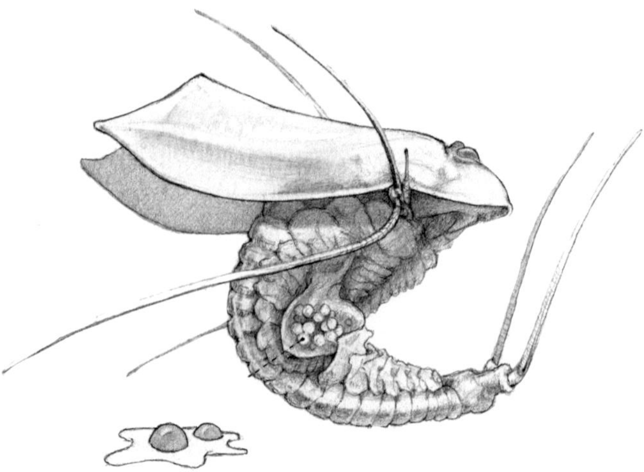

Triops eggs can withstand a lot, including drought, freezing temperatures, and many a digestive tract. These time capsules are stored in brood pouches on the eleventh pair of legs.

up in ceremonial ball courts of prehistoric Puebloan people at Wupatki National Monument, not far south of the Grand Canyon. They mobbed the gathering grounds of the Burning Man festival in the Black Rock Desert of far northwestern Nevada. From these two data points, you might guess that these desert shrimp love to crash parties.

They might have been a far more plausible protagonist than the hermit crab that Barbara Kingsolver accidentally brought home from the Bahamas in time to write about in her best-selling *High Tide in Tucson*. The probability that a hermit crab would survive in any home near Tucson other than Barbara's is one in several billion, while the probability of Triassic *Triops* surprising several Tucsonans is closer to one in a thousand. And the irony is that they clandestinely swim in small puddles all around desert dwellers in the Tucson Basin and in five thousand other settlements in arid lands. It is just that most residents don't take the time to look for them on the few days each year when they make cameo appearances in a nearby mud puddle.

Other than the fact that they couldn't care less whether any paparazzi arrive in time to shoot photos of them during their brief showings, the dinosaur shrimp are not only hospitable, but they also don't mind being caught nude as they lounge around their swimming pools. They welcome visits to watch them as they display their very distinctive traits.

First off, they are unusually perceptive of the goings-on in the world in a manner that humans can never be, thanks to their third eye. All three eyes can guide them to eat or reject the many plant and animal foods they consume, and to social gatherings of their kin. But their "third eye," hidden under a transparent shield covering their head, is highly sensitive to changes in light intensity and pattern. Found behind their eyes is a special sensor called a nuchal organ that guides them out of danger through its chemoreceptivity to the signals other aquatic animals transmit.

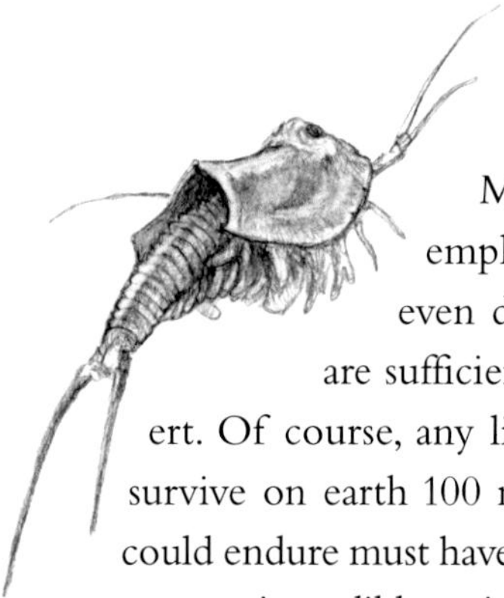

More than that, they are the prototypic exemplar of tenacity, waiting for years, perhaps even decades, before their eggs hatch after rains are sufficient to form deep pools of water in the desert. Of course, any lineage of tiny "dinosaur" mimics that can survive on earth 100 million years longer than *Tyrannosaurus rex* could endure must have the techniques of survival down pat. Their eggs are incredibly resistant to desiccation, driving rains, scorching summer temperatures, and icy winter blizzards. Although the *Triops* "mothers" bury their eggs deep in the mud, in slimy clay or slickrock cracks, the eggs are occasionally swept up by whirlwinds, dust devils, and gales that carry them long distances.

It is difficult to call their layers of eggs "mothers," in one sense, because few if any *Triops* eggs result from sexual reproduction, and there is no maternal care or "tending" after the eggs are laid. Some populations of *Triops* are hermaphrodites, and others are all females, laying eggs that do not develop through "mating," but through parthenogenesis, an umbrella term for several natural modes of asexual reproduction. In short, an embryo can grow in and then hatch out of an unfertilized egg.

Now, because of these out-of-the-ordinary modes of reproduction, many schoolchildren are curious to read about them, but adolescents are already ahead of their teachers because of their web-surfing skills. Hundreds of thousands of youths now grow out *Triops* each year in their schoolrooms and homes, purchasing kits from pet stores and biological supply houses regardless of whether they learn much about their unusual reproductive behaviors.

Calling them "aquasaurs" or "*Triops* trigons," schoolchildren rear them in aquaria, in bowls, or in plastic swimming pools, feeding them everything from Spam and bologna to Ritz crackers and barbecue potato chips. The children become entranced as they watch the shield shrimp collect tiny morsels of junk food by stroking and stirring their water until the food particles cling to the hairs on their limbs.

Triops are so good at foraging in murky water that in Japan, they are famed for their ability to control mosquitoes and are intentionally raised in rice paddies as biological control agents. Elsewhere, they are being auditioned for jobs controlling the *Culex* mosquitoes that vector the West Nile virus with the help of birds. Biological supply houses for both school science projects and biological control agents have now successfully bred "designer" aquasaurs that come in bright red or greenish-brown hues.

The kids have their priorities right. To watch a dinosaur shrimp swim around a glass bowl, or in a trickling stream of spring water, is such a beautiful sight: dazzled by the way it scurries along, its many limbs paddling in unison, propelled by the simple desire for a little bite to eat.

As we offer them our protracted attention, we meet the ancients, we honor our predecessors or ancestors on this planet, and we glimpse the primordial. We cheer for them, for they are still alive and kicking in our midst, at least 300 million years since they emerged as distinctive denizens of desert landscapes. While so many human empires have risen and then fallen in the same deserts over just a fraction of their time on earth, they play on an altogether different ballfield. And the name of their game is Persist, Persist, Swimmingly Persist.

DESERT PUPFISH

I live within one hundred yards of a restocked population of the Santa Cruz watershed desert pupfish that enjoys our half-acre pond. When the pupfish were initially released on our property, biologists from Arizona Game and Fish and U.S. Fish and Wildlife invited several Tohono O'odham youth visiting us to scoop the pupfish from buckets and liberate them into the cool waters of our Partners for Fish and Wildlife sanctuary. This novel pupfish may now be extirpated in most of its natural range but counts among its ancestors individuals from Monkey (or Manje) Springs, six miles to the north of our reservoir. Its shape, size, and habitat preferences may be markedly different from those of another pupfish that the Tohono O'odham are more likely to encounter in the homelands, the Quitobaquito pupfish, known only from the springs, channels, and pond at A'al Vaipia oasis in Organ Pipe Cactus National Monument, and in the Sonoyta River just to the south in Mexico. When my son was baptized in the oasis pond, he swam for a moment in the same waters with those pupfish.

Let me just confirm what you may already sense: I feel some kind of kinship with all seven of the pupfish species, as if we are kindred spirits dependent on the same waters. Among the tiniest of all fishes in western North America—with most adults barely reaching two or three inches in length—they have nevertheless achieved a certain fame. As Anna Mirocha has noted in her "Save the Weirdos" column for the Center for Biological Diversity, they are called pupfish because their swimming looks so playful to onlookers, as if they are inquisitive little canines. In fact, they do share several behavioral tendencies with puppy dogs, at least by Anna's criteria: they jerk around, nip, nuzzle, and patrol their territory like miniature watchdogs. And yet, the Spanish name found for these little squirts in the scientific literature, *cachorrito*, is entirely made up by the scientists themselves, simply a back translation of the English term pup. As far as I can tell, there is no baseball, basketball, or football team in either the United States or Mexico that has a pupfish or *cachorrito* as its mascot, although *chachorros* is often used as the name for teams playing *futbol del barrio*. That absence may be because most desert dwellers never actually glimpse pupfish in their habitats, since one species is extinct, two are dangerously rare, and the others are of federal conservation concern, largely because of widespread desiccation of their habitats in at least five states. That is ironic, because if left to their own devices, pupfish are very prolific, so much so that male pupfish get very blue when they can't find a mate! There is something wonderfully cryptic and tenacious about most pupfish. After decades of going by Quitobaquito Springs to offer my greetings to the little pups I've observed there over fifty years, I was worried that the draining of the pond by workers for the National Park Service to line its bottom with an impermeable mat might have negative effects on the little guys. To my pleasant surprise, the total pupfish population hidden in the cattails, rushes, and downed tree trunks in the pond was far higher than diligent scientific sampling had ever estimated. In addition, another kindred species, the Shoshone pupfish, has rebounded from near extinction to awesome abundance in a matter of decades. Some of the other pupfish species are still in "hot water," so to speak, but it is the rarity of their favored habitats that has rallied support for rather spectacular recovery efforts. Wouldn't you agree that we need to turn our attention to the charismatic minifauna of Planet Desert, as much as to its charismatic megafauna?

THREE

MOCHOMOS

Leaf-Cutter Ants as First Farmers

I am winding my way through all manner of thorny shrubs and spiny cacti to revisit some old friends. I am dodging cholla cacti, crucifixion thorn, mesquite, wolfberry, and prickly pear to reach my destination. It is hot, even within an hour of dusk, so I am trying to zigzag to where there is plenty of shade. I am endeavoring to stay as close to a dry watercourse called an arroyo, one of eleven washes with watered patches of cultivation out of dozens of the stream beds that cross the U.S.-Mexico border west of the Tohono O'odham Nation's reservation.

About forty years ago, I first became acquainted here with a colony of the descendants of the initial food-cultivating communities in the Americas. This colony began harvesting crops in the subtropical deserts and tropical forests millennia before other species did. They are among the northernmost rural communities of *Atta*

A creosote offering feeds that which feeds us.

mexicana, the famed Mexican leaf-cutter ants known as *mochomos* or *chicatanas* in Spanish-speaking reaches of the Americas.

More significantly, they are widely regarded as the first farmers in the present-day United States. *You got it*: they were already growing food before farming was considered cool. They have been featured in dozens of newspapers and magazines, including *The New York Times*, *Smithsonian*, *Science*, *Los Angeles Times*, and *Modern Farmer*. They are among the few widely heralded food producers in the desert still bringing in harvestable crops in the face of record-breaking summer temperatures and chronic water scarcity, without being propped up by government subsidies.

Whenever I get depressed about how many farmers in North America are going belly up due to accelerating climate change, I remember these former neighbors of mine, who have gone about their agricultural tasks uninterrupted for at least 20 million years. I once lived near where biologist Alex Mintzer surveyed Mexican leaf cutters over four decades. We both made pilgrimages to see them ever since, admiring their agricultural perseverance. The worker ants there are maintaining an agrarian tradition—of harvesting and cultivating perennials—that spans innumerable generations without depleting their primary inputs. I'm not particularly fond of such buzzwords, but more than any farmers I can think of, their agricultural practices are both sustainable and regenerative.

Somewhere in Mexico, between 65 and 30 million years ago, they adopted small-scale horticulture through an evolving mutualistic relationship with the wild progenitor of a particular fungus now called *Leucoagaricus gongylophorus*. This fungus began to colonize and transform the leaves and flowers the ants cut, bringing them back to their burrows to eat.

As the ants collected and piled up mounds of leaves, seeds, stems, buds, and flowers from subtropical forests, arid savannas, and deserts, the fungus fostered conditions that allowed for their fermentation, eliminating toxins and antinutritional factors. After

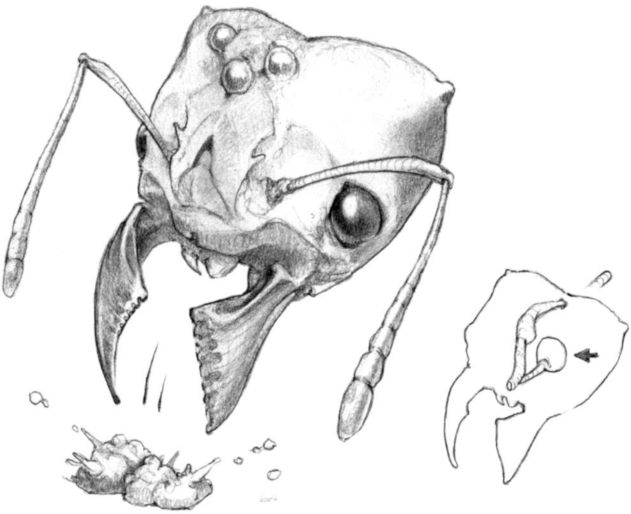

The infrabuccal pocket, a handy pouch in ants' mouths, is often used for gathering unwanted debris for disposal. But the young leaf-cutter queen uses it to save a piece of symbiotic fungus to seed a fungus garden in a new colony of her own.

who-knows-how-long, the ants gradually shifted to consuming the resulting fungus spores, not just the feedstock they grew on. I suppose we might liken it to giving up barely digestible raw soybeans to become a connoisseur of fermented miso paste. After millions of years of experimentation, the ants may have found other food sources that did not require fermentation, but they now survive by eating fungi exclusively.

By around 20 million years ago, as the ants domesticated the fungi, the ants and the fungi were full tilt into symbiotic relationships, the likes of which would make most farmers in North America look like isolationists, or Marlboro Men who preferred to "go it alone." What I saw being collected by the leaf cutters is now the foodstuff for the ants' symbiont, and this same species is no longer found "in the wild" outside the agrarian ant colonies in tropical and arid regions. That means that *Atta mexicana* and *Leucoagaricus gongylophorus*

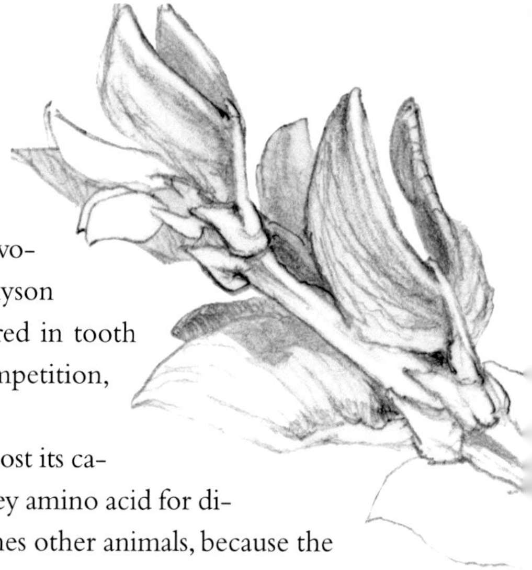

participate in an obligatory mutualism that is fitting for hot, challenging conditions, where early proponents of evolution like Darwin and Tennyson could only imagine "nature red in tooth and claw" predation and competition, not cooperation.

As for *Atta mexicana*, it has lost its capacity to make asparagine, a key amino acid for digesting raw foods that nourishes other animals, because the fungi provide all the nutrients it needs. Once this covenant of obligate mutualistic interaction was sealed, the *Atta-Leucoagaricus* symbiosis paved the way for a larger scale of perennial agriculture still practiced in Arizona and at least a dozen arid Mexican states. But at the same time, this symbiosis yielded enough ant biomass in the landscape that leaf cutters are now among the most widely eaten invertebrates in Mexico. They may not be your cup of formic acid, but I keep a jar of them, toasted ants mixed with salt, on the Formica counter in my kitchen, to use as a flavoring for foods and dusting on the glass rims of margaritas. (The formic acid is in the ant's venom.)

Oddy, the feedstock for the fungi comes primarily from the creosote bush, a heat- and drought-adapted perennial with circular clones that may live upward of eight thousand years. Creosote also remains the single most important medicinal plant for Indigenous cultures in the Sonoran, Mohave, and Chihuahuan deserts, so we might speculate whether *Atta* ants originated that ancient adage, "food is medicine." It is their nest disinfectant.

The fungi's mainstay, creosote, has huge medicinal value, in part because of the high antioxidant and antimicrobial content of its thirty-seven different volatile oils, which can help its consumers tolerate all manner of abiotic and biotic stresses. It probably knocks back bacterial competitors with the fungi themselves. Curiously, creosote is not considered a food by human dwellers in the desert because its fragrance is so astringent, yet it and eight of the other fifteen perennials that serve as secondary feedstocks for the *Atta-Leucoagaricus* partnership have been healing herbs for Indigenous cultures for upward of six to eight millennia. Oddly, only two annuals—a non-native grass called *Schismus*, and the native herb *Plantago insularis*—whose psyllium seeds maintain gastric motility, low blood sugar, and low cholesterol levels—play roles in desert leaf-cutter diets.

What seem to be the hallmarks of this profoundly successful agricultural society? I've pondered this a lot, but my responses are naïvely speculative. Females oversee the colonies, with the queen of the leaf cutters ascending to reside "on her throne" as the largest ant known in North America. Big Mama's workers include harvesters and soldiers that protect the supply chain as the harvest comes into the underground "growth chambers," but they only engage in defensive actions and never go on the offensive.

Alex Mintzer notes the nests are moved around within twelve-acre areas along ephemeral and intermittent watercourses, so that the harvesting area shifts on a decadal scale, almost like a rest-rotation cycle. And the feedstock is almost exclusively from perennial plants that need not be ripped out of the ground and replaced on an annual basis, thereby maintaining stability in both the surrounding vegetation and in the fungal community's nutritional uptake.

I feel humbled every time I visit this shrine to agricultural stability and resilience. For me, it does not matter that these farmers are not of my species; for as we learn to better employ the design concept of biomimicry, they may help us develop models that can be far more fruitful over the long haul than what most land-grant agricultural colleges offer their students.

I have also visited other colonies in the deserts of northwestern Mexico, where they remain known in Spanish as *mochomos*, a term also used as a nickname for nocturnal bootleggers of *mezcal bacanora* and sotol. These two-legged *mochomos* with sombreros set up their mobile, clandestine stills along the same arroyos and canyons where some of the ants make their harvests. In giving them a second nickname, *hormigas arrieras*, Sonorans also liken their diligence to drovers leading a mule train, whom old-time Westerners called mule skinners.

It seems that the appreciation shown toward *Atta* ants by their human neighbors is largely focused on the work they do above ground, not below, which may be out of sight and out of mind to most. But the work carrying leaves and flowers they see seems staggering: The leaf cutters consume a whopping 17 to 20 percent of all leaf litter in arid subtropical ecosystems, foraging out from their nests at least 140 yards in every direction to encompass harvesting areas of 12 acres or more. The average colony in Arizona collects about 440 pounds of bushy leaves, bracts, buds, and blossoms per year—not bad for ants that average less than a half inch in length.

Further south, in the arid subtropics of Mexico, the leaf cutters are called *chicatanas* and are valued for the tastes they impart to food and drink. They are gathered up, toasted, and mixed with sea salt to be placed on the rims of margarita cocktails or blended into guacamole. While U.S. tourists to Mexico may shudder at the thought of consuming ants or assume it is only a gimmick to lure in the gullible, millions of Mexicans still consume *chicatanas* every week, as they have done for upward of five to eight thousand years.

To be clear, I am not divulging all of this to convince you to take a nibble on *chicatanas* daily as some kind of superfood. I once watched, amused, as my vegan hero and friend from India, Vandana Shiva, rejected an entire plate of them at a restaurant featuring edible insects in Guadalajara, trying to explain to a flummoxed waiter that they, too, were animal flesh.

Instead, I am asking you to reflect upon the simple fact that something as small as a half-inch leaf-cutter ant has garnered culinary admiration, gastronomic awe, and agroecological respect from millions of people in Latin America. This is even though several *Attas* could fit on the claw of a grizzly bear, the eyelash of a jaguar, or the pin feather of a condor—the charismatic megafauna that attract most of the attention of aficionados of wildlife documentaries and adventure films.

How do we digest the fact that Mexican leaf-cutter ants have become *charismatic microfauna* for two very different constituencies: the media consumers of weird science who are fascinated by the life underground, and the tequila-rimmed-with-ant-salt consumers of popular Mexican culture who love them for their taste?

It may be one more example of how the views taken by Western scientists and consumers barely cross with those of Indigenous knowledge keepers and ant harvesters, for one is obsessed by the fungal underground and the other by what the *chicatanas* do above ground and among the spirits in a glass or gourd cup. We might all agree that *Atta mexicana* colonies are full of diligent, hardworking farm laborers. But that is about where the agreement ends. Most human farmers don't necessarily know that there may be farming ants beneath their feet, and most entomologists have never tasted the *sal de chicatana* on the rim of a glass of mezcal or tequila.

When we peer through the tequila glass darkly into this other world—one that my colleague, César Ojeda Linares, calls a "hidden biocultural landscape of food fermentation," perhaps even the slightest glance might enrich us all in unforeseen ways. In many cases, these glasses are neither half empty nor half full, all light or all darkness, for the ants and their microbes live out of sight, immersed in the creative tension between the two.

SAND TROUT

I have hooked one kind of sand trout on an island in the Mississippi River Delta, but never ones so sleek and beautiful as those reputed to be hiding deep in the dry sands of arroyos in the Sonoran Desert. They have wriggled around in the fish nets of the imaginations of many anglers who grew up catching trout in the lakes, rivers, and seas of America before they settled in the dry lands of Arizona and Sonora, where even a yard-wide ditch might be marked with a sign claiming that it is a fishable and navigable waterway. But out of such hydrological poverty, hope springs eternal, and that is why every bridge that spans the Río Santa Cruz has two or three transplanted fishermen reeling out their lines in dry riverbeds, waiting for a flash flood to appear and deliver to them the most voluptuous, glistening, dancing sand trout they could ever imagine. The major trouble that they face with climate change is that it is a toss-up whether the heat or drought will kill you first, or the fish you have been waiting for. Sadly the length of rainless periods this century has become so daunting that the sand trout remains in hibernation in dry riverbeds for years. By the time they emerge, when a gully washer comes along after a torrential monsoon storm, they have forgotten how to swim and therefore drown in the flood. I have proposed that sand trout be named Arizona's most endangered but beloved fish, but the State Legislature is still debating the merits of my proposal. If it ever passes the House and Senate, should we make sand trout almondine our state dish?

RAZORBACK SUCKER

When fish the size of my three-year-old daughter once swam through prehistoric Hohokam canals, the razorback sucker was among the most frequent fare harvested in the largest Indigenous irrigation system in North America. Its bones still appear in trash heap samples that salvage archaeologists dig up in the ancient canals buried beneath Metropolitan Phoenix. Razorbacks once grew to a yard in length and weighed up to thirteen pounds, a size that remains respectable in the eyes of most Western anglers today. But get this: They were once so common throughout the Salt, Gila, and Colorado watersheds in the West that their bones and teeth are among the most common animal remains uncovered by zooarchaeologists. Where they frequented the main ditches of the Pima Indians in historic times, elderly Pima men described with some flair this fish, which they call *o'omuni*: "It has a yellowbelly [and] looks like trout, more or less, but the front of its back has a high bump, and its tail tapers thin, so that it comes down like this . . ." as Bert Cooley once showed me and Amadeo Rea, shaping with his hands the low spot between the hump and the tail. For Sylvester Matthias, the *o'omuni* sucker's actions were particularly memorable: "*O'omuni* behave like carp, not [like fish that move] in schools. They are fast and stay on the side where the river is cutting under the bank, so they can go under it and hide. And they are slippery." That's right: their scales are so deeply embedded in their leathery skin that these suckers feel smooth and slimy, not rough and scaly. Their bodies are a lovely olive brown on top, but a paler, creamier yellow underneath. I once spent a few days and nights in the Grand Canyon monitoring another sucker that the razorbacks occasionally mate with, the flannelmouth, so that hybrids occur in some streams. The adults congregated in the backwaters of eddies that form near river bends and were quite easy to net and measure. But overall, they love dynamic, flowing stream waters, so much so that the damming of desert rivers has sounded a death knell for most species of suckers. The razorback that was once among the largest and most conspicuous suckers in all of North America is but a shadow of its former glory. It may well be that the Hohokam were among the few riverine tribes in the West that practiced a kind of informal aquaculture in their irrigation canals, opening them up when river flows were high with snowmelt, then closing sections off with slats of wood and reeds so that the fish would adjust to the warmer, shallower water. Young men, girls, and boys would leap into the canal, make a splash, catch the suckers, and throw them up onto dry ground for their sisters and brothers to sequester in baskets and pots. But why does it sound so strange when we learn the prehistoric dwellers of the Sonoran and Mohave deserts once had "all-you-can-eat" mesquite-grilled fish many months of the year, in places where fish fries now feature finfish from the ocean that were brought in from hundreds of miles away?

WALKING CATFISH

Although they are native to Asia, from the Malay Archipelago to Sri Lanka, these ambulatory interlopers were first spotted by the eighty-two-mile All-American Canal west of Yuma in southeast California in the 1960s. At least two more were spotted in the canal over the following decade. Their unusual capacity to use their pectoral spines to pivot and exhibit forward-lunging movements over gravel and sand has allowed them to leave acequias and shallow side channels of rivers. They travel overland across muddy roads and levees during thunderstorms. This true catfish—also naturalized in Florida—is not to be confused with another wet-finned walker. The northern snakehead fish, or *Channa argus,* was seen in California as recently as 2023 and dubbed the "frankenfish" by the invasive species biologists who dread its arrival in the West from East Asia. Neither should it be confused with bagre San Joaquin, a catfish au gratin served with mushrooms and shrimp in much of Latin America. Because there are now so many walking catfish videos posted on YouTube, Vimeo, and TikTok, don't you think our charismatic carousers of the *Clarias batrachus* species should have their own award category in the Oscars, vying for the best lead role by an outstanding catfish?

FOUR

THE SILK MOTH

Its Resonant Cocoon and Its Jumping Bean

I am lucky enough to live in one of the only two counties in the United States where one of the largest silk moths in North America frequents. The *cincta* silk moth (*Rothschildia cincta*) has a wingspan of nearly five inches, which makes it nearly as large as many bats. Like bats, they are largely nocturnal, although they mate in the *madrugada* or dawning hours of the summer, and the females then lay their eggs just before dusk.

They are part of a group of moths called saturniids, which all have very poor eyesight as caterpillars, but this species "makes up" for that as adults with four pale, translucent wing spots that look like enormous eyes. Their folk name in Spanish reflects this image: *cuatro espejos* (the "four-mirrored" moth). Curiously, one of its most peculiar traits is that its mouth really can't be opened due to the proboscis protruding over it, so the adult moths neither eat nor drink during their short lifespan of five to twenty days.

But the neighbors' odd homes
hid their silk on the inside.

Once every few summers, I find a cluster of these moths below the nightlight at our front door, and I am dazzled by their dark red or chocolate brown wings punctuated by these wise-looking eyes. The adults do not stay around our rural neighborhood for very long, but I am always reminded of where they live in the Sonoran Desert by the large, silky cocoons they leave behind on a discrete set of shrubs in these arid landscapes. It is the cocoon of this moth that has found its way into the legends and folk culture of a half-dozen Indigenous nations in the binational Sonoran Desert.

I first came upon these cocoons not in the wilds of Sonora, but in a barrio in the Old Pueblo of the Yoeme community (known to outsiders as the Pascua Yaqui). The Yoemem graciously welcome their neighbors to Lenten ceremonies every year. I began going to Easter ceremonies at Pascua Vieja in the heart of downtown Tucson when I turned twenty-four and have been in attendance whenever possible ever since. And one of the first sounds a newcomer hears as she or he approaches the ceremonial grounds after dark on Holy Saturday is the sound of *sapo tenevoim*—leg rattles made from the cocoons of the *cuatro espejos* moth, and one other, the *calleta* silk moth.

Forty to a hundred cocoons may be tied to a strand of rawhide or agave fiber and wrapped around each leg of a Yaqui *maaso* deer dancer or a *pahk'ola* clown dancer; each cocoon has a handful of pebbles taken from ant mounds embedded in it before it is tied onto the strand. As a deer dancer shuffles along a dirt dance floor, shaking gourd rattles in each hand, the accompanying sound from the cocoons is reminiscent of the rattling of a sidewinder, Mohave, or western diamondback snake. Others have suggested that it is much more pleasant than the warning of a rattlesnake, akin to the shudder and shimmer of cottonwood or aspen leaves as gentle rains come on. Still others contend that the sound is hypnotic, sending them into a trancelike state that heightens the intensity of the ceremonies they are witnessing.

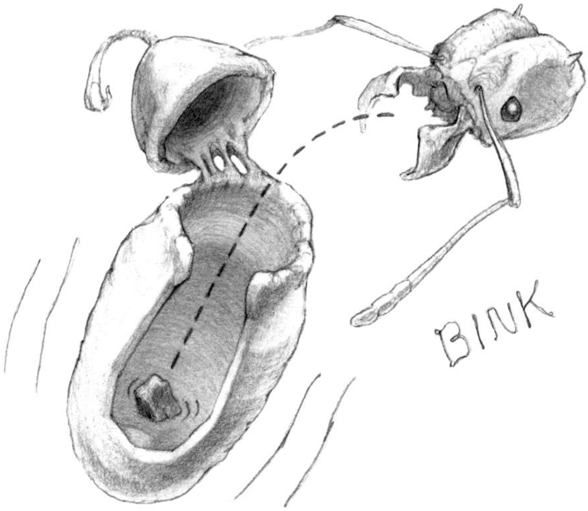

"[E]ach cocoon has a handful of pebbles taken from ant mounds embedded in it before it is tied onto the strand."

As my friend Felipe Molina has beautifully described, those Yoeme individuals who participate in these ceremonies are inclined to offer a sense of deep respect or gratitude (known as *yo'oriwa*) for the *sapo tenevoim*, for they know that these cocoons were once the homes of the silk moths. As Felipe once explained to me, even to harvest a cocoon off a host plant for use in making the rattles, the forager must express his sense of *yo'oriwa* by leaving an offering or prayerfully talking to the host plant.

Although I have been fortunate enough to be hosted by Felipe and his relatives for Easter Week ceremonies on the other side of the border in Pótam, Sonora, the Yaqui pueblos are not the only places I have witnessed silk moth rattles in action. The Mayo kin of the Yaqui, who call themselves the Yoremem, also used them in ceremonies, as do their neighbors in the Sierra Madre above the Río Yaqui and Río Mayo, the Guarijio, and the Tohono O'odham in Arizona.

When I have been in all-night festivals of the Guarijio at Mesa Colorada near the Sonora-Chihuahua border, both Mayo and Guarijio pascola dancers clown around with their cocoon rattle leggings, offering percussion that follows any joke they throw out into the crowd. But I have also offered leggings of *tenevoim* rattles to Comcaac and Tohono O'odham pascola dancers who can hardly find the cocoons in their homelands any longer. Older reports on the use of silk moth cocoons by Indigenous dancers once affirmed that they were only used in Sonora by tribes in the Uto-Aztecan language family, but the Comcaac are an exception, since they belong to a different language family. The O'odham communities in Arizona are another exception to this rule, since they live in Arizona at the northernmost edges of *cincta* silk moth distribution.

Deer dancers and their leggings of silk moth cocoons are now internationally revered, in part because they have become an icon of Indigeneity throughout Mexico and the world through some rather superficial reenactments of the ritual by professional ballerinas. Over more than half a century, the touring troupe of the Ballet Foklórico de México brought a highly dramatized version of the deer dance to tens of thousands of Mexicans, Americans, and Europeans. There are huge statues of deer dancers placed along Mexico's interstate highways, and the most famous hot sauce with wild Sonoran chiltepins in it was named "Salsa Yaqui." Its label has prominently featured a deer dancer with cocoon leggings for more than seventy-five years and is sold on both sides of the U.S.-Mexico border.

I have found silk moth cocoons on desert plants like limber bush near the Baboquivari Mountains just west of Tucson, and on a bush that grows widely in the desert called *goma de Sonora*, but the plant from which I've collected most silk moth cocoons is known in Mexico as *yerba de la flecha*, for its milky sap is toxic and is used as an arrow poison and fish stupefaction agent. Perhaps the first European killed by being shot with a poison arrow in the Sonoran Desert was a soldier who accompanied Francisco Vázquez de Coronado through the Río Sonora to the headwaters of the Río Santa Cruz just south of the border. But in my heart, this plant is less of a toxic threat and more of a gift to dwellers and visitors of the borderlands.

My affection for this prominent host of silk moth caterpillars and cocoons leapt into my heart at an earlier age, long before I knew about the silk moth and its relationship to the diverse Indigenous peoples of the desert and adjacent arid subtropical scrublands. It belongs to the genus of subtropical plants named *Pleradenophora*, which includes the various Mexican jumping beans known in Spanish as *brincadores* (jumpers). My old mentor Richard Felger coined the name "Arizona jumping bean" for the northernmost member of this group, *Pleradenophora bilocularis*, that reaches all the way up to South Mountain in Metropolitan Phoenix.

From the 1940s through the 1960s, jumping beans were sold throughout the United States in little boxes with a cartoon on top that depicted the bean with a sombrero leaping up out of the desert. On my first trip west with my Lebanese American family, we bought several boxes of jumping beans from a Mexican curios store in southern Colorado.

To be clear, the triangular seeds of *Pleradenophora bilocularis* are not true beans, nor do they gyrate on their own volition. They must be infested by the small larvae of a moth (*Cydia deshaisiana*) to be able to leap up from a tabletop or from a child's hand. To increase their jumpiness so their owners don't get bored, it is best to place them in sunlight, so they warm up and awaken from their slumber.

All the way back from Colorado to the Great Lakes, I was mesmerized by the little jumping beans we had received as gifts. It was my first glimpse of the many contributions that Mexico's biodiversity and cultural diversity have offered the world at large, and I remain grateful for that. I was so enthralled that when my own bean stopped wriggling for a while, I would steal my brothers' boxes, put my sleepy bean in one of theirs, and sequester their beans until they began to wake up from their naps.

During the era when Mexican jumping beans were the rage among American adolescents—long before Pokémon and Dungeons & Dragons—rural Sonorans could make a decent living collecting the moth-infested seeds of this shrub for export, and the cocoons for local use by deer dancers.

I would argue that many children who might otherwise be prone to expressing the behaviors associated with attention-deficit disorders may be calmed without the use of medications by letting them watch the moth larvae do all the tumbling, jumbling, turning, and jiving in their hands. I make such an assertion only because I was one of those attention-deficit-hyperactivity-disordered children who was simultaneously tranquilized and enthralled by my relationship with jumping beans.

Alas, climate change began to desiccate many of the host plant populations that silk moths and their kin inhabited. Worse yet, the U.S. government began to help Mexico control drug production by spraying the fields with deadly paraquat herbicides, which not only dried up cannabis plants in the fields, but also silk moth host plants beyond the margin. The drift of herbicides wiped out silk moths and their host plants on tens of thousands of acres where jumping beans of *sapo tenevoim* cocoons were once collected, and these cottage industries crashed.

The story of the silk moth and the jumping bean host plants reminds me that there are marvels in the world that leap up all around us, thanks to the intricate interactions between plants and animals, not from a species in isolation. To put it baldly, if there is no host plant, there is no silk moth, no cocoon, no entrancing rattle emanating from the leggings of the deer dancer. If there are no *Cydia* moth larvae, there is no jumping bean, and no child struck silent by rapture.

Let me be bold enough to say that I do believe in the magic embedded in all of this. One time, while walking along the Río Mayo

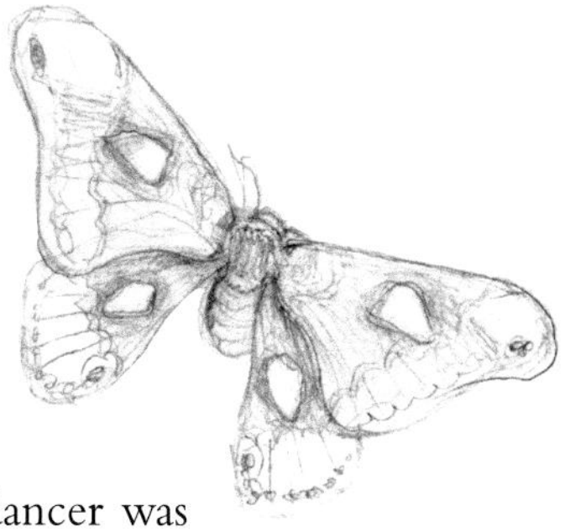

floodplain with a cottonwood forest on one side of me and a field of native crops on the other side, I heard rattling not far from me, and because it was too loud to be a rattlesnake, I instantly realized that a deer dancer was shuffling around with his cocoon leggings on somewhere close by. As I started to walk into the cottonwood grove to see if there was a ceremony going on, an Indigenous farmer came up from behind me and stopped me in my tracks.

"I'm sorry, you can't go over there, the *maaso* is practicing his dance for a ceremony that will begin tonight. This young man is so focused on his *manda*—his sacred obligation as a deer dancer—that he sometimes turns into a real deer over there. Once, I accidentally saw him transform himself while he was practicing, and it shook me to my bones. I don't think a stranger to our culture can make full sense of that. Instead, why don't you join us tonight at the fiesta, when all will be allowed to see the spiritual power that he carries?"

COLORADO RIVER PIKEMINNOW

These bronze-backed behemoths of the Colorado River watershed are as immense as an imaginary super-fish, and they are the real deal. They have been called everything from the lions of the river to bonytail salmons, Verde River trout, and formerly, by the racist and misogynistic term *squawfish*. Over their 3 million years on earth, they have outlived mammoths, mastodons, and most political parties. Forty-year-old torpedo-shaped males once achieved weights of one hundred pounds and lengths of five to six feet, yet most current pikeminnows look like juvenile delinquents by comparison. It turns out that these freshwater wonders are among the largest minnows in the world. If that sounds like an oxymoron, it is because our word *minnow* comes from the Latin *minutus* to refer to small objects, but small they are not. Once one is hooked, it might take two or three men to wrestle down into a dory in its Colorado River haunts. These *pescados* were hauled over to Lees Ferry to be the featured catch for an eight-course Christmas dinner in 1889, served with oxtail soup, roast beef, and turkey for all of Robert Brewster Stanton's crew members to enjoy for the holiday. Those explorers set out on that ill-fated survey to find a safe route for running a railroad line straight through the entire Grand Canyon, a notion crazy enough to make any

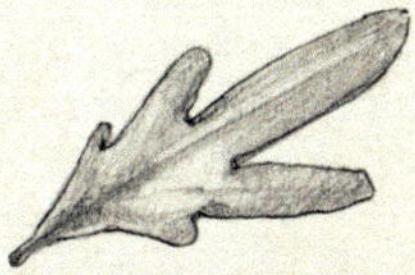

pikeminnow lover flip out. As a flagship species of the Colorado River Basin, how the red river goes, so goes the pikeminnow. Its population demise was hastened by the onset of construction of the Hoover Dam in 1930 and the Glen Canyon Dam in 1956, for those engineering feats tripped up the migration of fish that ran the gamut between the canyon and the river delta from May to early July. Alas, the last wild-born, free-running Colorado River pikeminnow found between Glen Canyon Dam and Lake Powell was spotted near the mouth of Havasu Creek in 1976, then *zip*. In all my time rafting in the red river, I never encountered one, yet I dreamed of seeing "so excellent a fish" of my own size. Damnable dams continue to constrain pikeminnow movements from the Upper Colorado all the way to the confluence with the Sea of Cortés, so the current runs are isolated from one another by reservoirs full of silt, beer cans, and little else. Should the movement called Raise the River ever ramp up enough to warrant the complete removal of big dams from the river, wouldn't you be willing to buy a ticket for a riverside seat to see them race from the headwaters of the Green River on the Continental Divide in Wyoming, down to the delta in Baja California, so you could tell of *the one that got away*?

FIVE

ARIZONA BARK SCORPIONS

More Swing than Sting

Sometimes, legends come upon us; we do not have to go looking for them.

It is therefore not surprising that we don't initially comprehend the fantastic significance of the moment when such sage beings surprise us on our quest for the mythic creatures of the Sonoran Desert. That is what happened one evening just after dark, when Alaskan storyteller and ethnozoologist Richard "Nels" Nelson barged into our house in Desemboque del Sur, with news that three sagacious creatures had crept up on us, just beyond our back door.

Nels was shouting, "Come here quick, this is amaaaaaazing!"

It was a thrill to have an Arctic explorer in the desert with us, for it seemed that everything Nels observed on the arid coast was throwing him off kilter and exciting him. Were the heat and dryness getting to him? To find out, my wife, Laurie, and I leapt up and

I venture out once the daystar
has left my cholla's vents.

scrambled to follow him out the back door. I vaguely recalled that decades before, Nels had spent an entire summer at Arizona State's Poison Control Center in Tempe, but it did not occur to me that he might be leading us toward venomous animals.

But when we reached the seaward side of our cabin, he waved us toward our rather rustic outhouse behind it. That's when we first sensed that we might be witnessing something downright creepy.

"Quick, gather around inside, you won't regret it," Nels whispered, clicking on the LED light to his headlamp.

"W-w-wait a minute, Nels," I stammered, "The tradition—the custom—here in Sonora is that only one person uses an outhouse at a time. It might seem indelicate to our neighbors if they saw three of us enter it together."

"But there are times when we must put etiquette aside, and this is a chance of a lifetime!" Nels responded.

"You have an unprecedented opportunity . . ." he continued, "as I did just a few seconds ago as I was sitting down, to see a *bark scorpion, a tarantula, and a black widow spider together!* They are all hovering within feet of the toilet seat inside there. Imagine that! Three of the most venomous invertebrates in the Sonoran Desert, and they decided to make a joint appearance just as I was pulling down my pants!"

He was right, of course. Why should we hesitate? As the three of us peered into the outhouse, Nels's LED lamp's ultraviolet beam flashed onto the bark scorpion, which fluoresced into a beautiful hue of whitish blue. The scorpion wagged its tail at us, flaunting its zinc-reinforced pincers and stinger, as if delighted by the size of the prey that had just come within its reach.

We were captivated! That's when we became the fools who rush in where angels fear to tread. As we crowded around the commode, the bark scorpion, the tarantula, and the black widow froze in place less than the length of a shoe on either side of it, looking rather nonplussed. Under other circumstances, either of these spiders might turn to bite a scorpion with its fangs, but then again, bark scorpions have been known to take down these eight-legged arthropods, stunning them with their stingers.

For them, it's an arachnid-eat-arachnid world we live in. By the very sight of them looming in the lavatory together, Richard had been struck with something akin to spiritual awe.

"I can't believe our luck: It's like witnessing the Holy Trinity of desert sting! It makes me weak in the knees!"

His enthusiasm bubbled over like a plugged toilet bowl.

"It is indeed a rare moment to behold," I conceded. "It's like arriving in an arena just in time for a triple-header of pro wrestlers . . . Three venomous creatures all primed to engage in a gallant fight to the death!"

At this point, Laurie was rolling her eyes, slowly inching backward away from the latrine. "Excuse me, boys, but this is . . . Too much."

Soon after, we all backed out of the privy, overwhelmed by the stirring scene and the not-so-sublime odor of it all. I took a deep breath of fresh air, then glanced around to see if our Comcaac neighbors had witnessed our irreverent behavior. Luckily we had gone unnoticed.

We ambled back through the kitchen door and pulled out our field journals to register this unprecedented sight into our life lists. We had responded swiftly, but cautiously enough to avoid getting stung. And so we celebrated our good fortune by cracking open a bottle of root beer to toast our stroke of luck.

Of course, not everyone sees such a spine-tingling moment as a blessing. I remember when my buddy, Bill Risner, once let us rent his beachside home in Kino Bay for a week. Before departing, he first walked around each bedroom with an ultraviolet light to show us where all the glowing scorpions rested within reach of where we ourselves would rest our weary heads. After Risner had intentionally ramped up my dread for bark scorpions, he winked as he tossed me his house keys:

"I hope you will sleep safe and sound here tonight!"

If I remember correctly, twenty-four scorpions lit up as he said that. Of course, Risner was right: the presence of scorpions is nothing to sneeze at. One must become preternaturally alert to their presence or the worst might happen. Arizona bark scorpions are the most venomous of all scorpions in North America, and hundreds of thousands of stings are recorded in emergency rooms each year, though few ever prove fatal.

Bark scorpions share a few of their neurotoxins with tarantulas and black widows, but each species has its own blend of nasty chemicals that are used to stun prey, disable competitors, or repel other predators pursuing them. Compared with these spiders, bark scorpions rely more heavily on chlorotoxins to excite the neurons and neurotransmitters of their prey. Through their stingers, they inject cysteine-rich peptides that can royally disrupt their victims' nervous systems. Arizona bark scorpions also employ hyaluronidase, an enzyme they share with tarantulas, that breaks down proteins in the flesh of their captives and then serves as a spreading factor for most neurotoxins in the scorpion venom, since they don't necessarily diffuse through the bloodstream of the victim all the time.

Unfortunately, a few years before I had my own exposure to bark scorpion venom, I had to watch as my seven-year-old son, Dusty, writhed as his finger throbbed with a sting. He was helping me unload a pickup truck load of fired bricks we had brought across the border from Sonoyta, Sonora. Each row of bricks had a thin layer of straw and hay below it as a buffer for the ride on the dirt road up to the international port of entry. I simply had not thought about this thin matrix of loose material serving as a perfect habitat for arachnids of any kind.

As we were unloading the second or third layer of bricks from the bed of the truck, I saw Dusty shake his hand as if he had lodged a splinter in his finger. Then he let out a little howl, and I realized

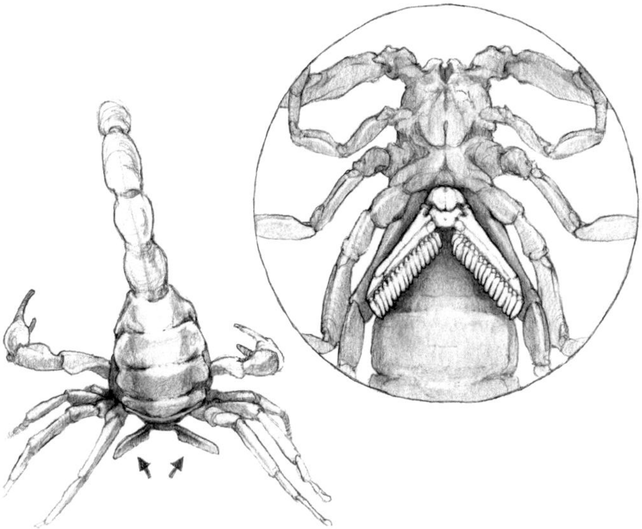

Near the center of a scorpion's underbelly are a pair of comblike organs called pectines. These are swept along the ground to sense vibrations and to help create a mental map of smells, pheromones, and textures.

that he had been hurt by something other than a mesquite thorn or cactus spine. The incision was not visible to us, but his skin reddened around it, and it was obviously throbbing. He whimpered some but was either bravely stoic about it all, or he had received only a small dose of venom with the sting. We elevated his arm, iced it as best as we could, and led him to a bed in a darkened room where he could sleep it off. Within about six hours, the throbbing had stopped, and the pain had lessened. Nevertheless, I was so sad and anxious enough about his being wounded on my watch that I carefully checked his symptoms every few hours for the next two days.

My own scorpion stings came to me twice in the middle of the night in Patagonia, Arizona, once on my leg and another time on my shoulder while I was sleeping. Each time, I felt sharp nerve pain, followed by several hours of numbing, throbbing heat, pulsating around a reddened, swollen area where no puncture wound could be seen. Within an hour of the first injection of scorpion venom, I felt nauseous and short of breath and had the disturbing sense of being sickened if not poisoned. My heart rate seemed to hasten, perhaps as a sign of mild tachycardia.

The second time, I became hyperalert after being rudely awakened and desperately combed through the bedclothes trying to confirm whether it was a scorpion or a spider that had come to bed with me. I glimpsed something scurrying away with movements that belied a scorpion or vinegarroon, but I never smelled the "vinegar" that the nonvenomous candidate reliably leaves in the air. As I wrote down all my symptoms and compared them with those on websites, the bark scorpion emerged as the prime suspect. Nevertheless, it was difficult for me to be sure about anything at all when my sleep had been interrupted in the middle of the night, for the initial intensity of pain made me somewhat delirious.

Then there came the "long tail" of more subtle effects of being envenomated, ones featuring tingling, twitching, and stinging, but also a tedious tongue spasm. Yet overall, they were no longer that unpleasant. I called to mind a report about grasshopper mice being injected with bark scorpion venom, some brief note I may have read in the pages of the journal *Science*. All I could remember was that the mice had developed some chemical resistance to scorpion venom, acting as if they were largely oblivious to the pain, except for obsessively licking their paws until the numbing effects had probably simmered down.

If I recall correctly, in small doses, scorpion venom may impart an analgesic effect in certain mammals after being injected into their tissues, rather than causing a toxic effect. I couldn't help but wonder whether my dose of venom around the puncture point of the sting had slid past the level of nerve pain stimulation and into one of calming relief. That effect occurred hours after the pain had peaked, long after my vision was no longer blurry and my propensity for drooling had trickled to a halt. I don't recall feeling any urge to lick my paws, but I was still not very prone to such cravings anyway.

It struck me that almost all the attention we shower on scorpions revolves around the first few hours of a usually unpremeditated sting, but we exhibit little curiosity about the rest of their lives. After all, their venom is not typically intended for animals of our girth and height, but for the smallest of neighbors, ones that offer scorpions a rather modest diet: beetles, centipedes, cockroaches, crickets, katydids, spiders, and termites. In essence, bark scorpions help regulate the populations of invertebrates that we may consider as "pesty" as scorpions themselves.

If we open our eyes to observe their daily and seasonal activities, most of us will find a little tenderness for these desert neighbors of ours. I once heard an Indigenous elder speak with affection for the way mothering bark scorpions nudge their newborn scorplings onto what I recognized as the dorsal portion of their tan exoskeleton, so that they can "piggyback-ride" for protection until the moment they go through their first molt.

They remain rather social for most of the five to seven years they are alive, touching one another while sleeping in groups of twenty to forty and cuddling compactly during winter nights when temperatures plummet all around them. They find each other—especially potential mates—by leaving pheromone "vapor trails" of enticing chemicals for one another. But they also rely on sensory organs called *slit sensilla* that can alert them to nearby movements of friends and foes, or detect (and delight them with) the slightest breeze of fresh air.

The vapor trails of pheromones are what prompt them to participate in the mating tango that the French call *promenade à deux*. As the males and females come to face one another, the males clasp the females' pincers with their own, or more properly, they grip the pedipalp chelae of their potential mate. They then test one another's strength, each pushing forward toward their partner, or resisting the other's force. The male arouses the female by caressing her mouth parts with something akin to a kiss or a little sting. It's a bit of a tango!

The couple may even lock their pincers together in a manner that begins to move both in an intertwined spiral or circle, slowly whirling like Sufi dervishes for as long as ten to fifteen minutes a dance. But their tango slows to a halt when the male deposits his sperm package to the ground and holds the female tightly so that she hovers over this spermatophore, then drops down on it long enough to take in his sperm. The "spent" males sometimes die immediately after mating.

These are behaviors that the many species of bark scorpions have likely been engaged in for the last 50 to 60 million years, since they arrived on dry land. But some may be vestiges of ancestral behaviors that their predecessors first practiced at sea some 430 million years ago on "planet ocean." They remind us that scorpions transcend their stereotype of venomous gangs of terrorists hiding under every pillow, crook, and cranny in our homes and patios.

I am constantly saddened by how we as humans tend to objectify and vilify others, unlike ourselves, into callous monsters when they are far more complex than that. It has become clear to me that bark scorpions have lives far richer than the one morphological feature of theirs that most of us obsessively focus on, the presence of the telson "stingers" on their tails. Oddly, many humans confer more admirable qualities to the stellar constellation named Scorpius than we do to the very animal for which it is named. Since the era of the Roman Empire, the Latin word *scorpius* has essentialized these complex beings into nothing more than "creatures with a burning sting."

And yet, there is an aperture into a more nuanced view of scorpions. It is embedded in the ancient astrological traditions associated with "reading" the zodiac: that those who are born under the sign of Scorpio have an acute "sixth sense," an emotional depth, an intense and passionate capacity for expressiveness, a strong determination, and a rather secretive, mysterious element hidden in the way they live on earth. But why has that particular set of attributes been associated with Scorpio for centuries? Are they derived from traits that our ancestors associated with living, breathing scorpions here on earth? Could they have possibly been aggregated from observations made by the ancients who offered attention to scorpions themselves over many centuries and millennia? Did the ancients "see" something in these creatures that we no longer see, especially by rationalists who simply write off anything associated with astrology as a bunch of hooey?

For that matter, are we simply afraid for some reason to grant "personhood" to scorpions? Would the ethical act of treating scorpions' status as sentient beings be an outrageous affront to "empirical, secular, materialistic, objective science," threatening to lead our society back into the "mire" of superstition and pseudoscience?

I remain suspicious of such arguments, after hearing similar ones used to blatantly disregard the value of Indigenous, Eastern, and Islamic sciences, dismissing them as hogwash, old wives' tales, fables, and fallacies. Some Western academic scientists feel that other cultures' spiritual and ethical values have distorted or corrupted views of nature, leading them away from a more rational, *science-based* view of reality, as if there is only one legitimate brand of science.

While I am personally not a fan of astrology, I remain intellectually curious about how and why certain characteristics have become metaphors associated with Scorpius and scorpions. Could it be that they offer us other windows into the worlds of scorpions that are worthy of our reflection and consideration?

While we deliberate that question, Arizona bark scorpions wag their tails to one side, then to the other of their lithe, agile bodies, in an entrancing manner. They might alert us to the fact that their many gifts may be at least as interesting as their stings.

SANTA CATALINA ISLAND RATTLE-LESS RATTLESNAKE

When I have boated out toward the islands in the Gulf of California to fish and camp with Comcaac, Sonoran, or Californio friends, there is often a worrisome moment just after we arrive on shore to set up camp. They warn me that there may be rattle-less rattlesnakes on the island where we have landed, and they fastidiously clear the area around where they place their sleeping bags and urge me to do the same. Some of them place a ring of jet-black cobbles two feet out from where their sleeping bags will lie, as if the snakes will not be enticed to cross hot rocks during the night. At first I was amused by their dread of such poisonous pit vipers, because the only scientifically documented site for the rare rattle-less species is Santa Catalina Island, off the coast of the Baja California peninsula. And yet fishermen who frequently camp out in the Midriff archipelago of the Gulf insist they have encountered such aberrant forms on other islands. One Comcaac fisher, Roberto Camposano, described to me how some of the snakes on Isla Ángel de la Guarda and Isla San Esteban are functionally unable to make warning signals due to a deformation in the rattle segments that allows them to slip off the tail. On those two islands—each known for its endemic species of pit vipers—he has killed dozens of these soundless snakes, bringing them home to the mainland to process their bones rather than their button-like rattle segments. Roberto and his companions shuddered as they explained that nothing feels worse than trying

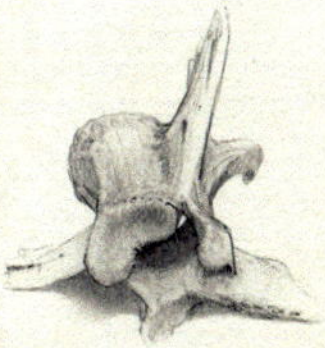

to deal with a rattlesnake cuddling up on their sleeping bags in the middle of the night when it had arrived unannounced. Having found sidewinders and diamondbacks hiding in my own bedroll just before turning in for the night, I can assure you that even when they suddenly sound off with a warning, there is no place in the world that you would rather *not* be. It is possible that the same evolutionary factors that selected for the snakes on Santa Catalina to give up their rattles for tiny buttons at the end of their tails might be active influences on the other islands: a paucity of predators that might be scared away by rattling; insular "poverty" and resource scarcity that discouraged investments in jewelry and baby toys; and good ol' genetic drift. But only on Santa Catalina is there a bona fide species—not just a few individuals or a breeding population—that no longer shakes, rattles, or rolls. The species in question—*Crotalus catalinensis*—is slender but fairly long, reaching nearly two and a half feet from nose to button. It is considered critically endangered on a global scale, but is that because the island has very little optimal habitat in its seventy-five square miles for such snakes, or is it because ophidiophobia—a hard-wired trepidation regarding snakes—has prompted so many of the island's historic visitors to brandish machetes and maul any snake in sight?

SIX

AJOLOTE

The Five-Toed Mole Lizard—Oracle of Orifices

You will likely never see one in the wild, so let me help you imagine what five-toed mole lizards look like on the Baja California peninsula and in a small patch of Sonora. Do not confuse this northern *ajolote* with the now-endangered salamander named *axolote*, once common around Mexico City; they are of a different feather. If you were ever granted the good fortune of glimpsing an *ajolote* suddenly unearthed, emerging from its burrows after a torrential rain and flash floods, you might be struck by this wormlike reptile's lack of hind legs. And yet, unlike other members of its family, it retains stubby front legs that look like shovels, clamps, or paddles, capable of clawing into any soft material placed before them.

Its blunt, tapered head is ergonomically designed to push forward into sand and gravel as its front legs and tail churn forward while

Swimming through a slice of earth with buried eyes.

it excavates tunnels. At first its skin looks smooth and pink like a baby's hind end, but then you notice that it is segmented into sections reminiscent of corrugated cardboard. Each of these sections can independently stretch its length to inch forward, but it can also contract like an accordion.

This concertina-like locomotion is called *peristalsis*, a wavelike contraction and expansive relaxation of muscles that results in a rather radical shift, forcing the entire musculature to push forward symmetrically. This rhythmic pattern of alternating contractions and extensions is much like the way your food moves from your esophagus down through the intestines. But in this case, it is the journey of a fossorial reptile with keen senses into the underworld, not the descent of foodstuffs into the underbelly.

Now here is the kicker: to have a head that moves like an auger to push sand, silt, and pebble out of the way as it excavates tunnels, this lizard has had to buffer its rudimentary eyes under a protective shield of scales. It can perceive patterns of lightness and darkness but has little capacity for visual image formation. While some claim this makes a mole lizard virtually blind, that may be an overstatement, for it can detect motion before its very eyes wherever it slithers in its shadow world. It might be best to regard *ajolotes* as the undisputed champions of "tunnel vision."

Similarly, its ears do not look as fully developed as those of other lizards. They, too, are concealed by a layer of scales that deftly allows the capture and transfer of any sound vibrations to the cochlea, the spirally coiled chamber inside the temporal bone that receives sounds in the form of vibrations. There these vibrations are converted into nerve impulses that are passed on to the mole lizard's brain to interpret.

The acuity of *ajolote* hearing is among the highest audio capacity of any lizards sampled by scientists so far. The *ajolote* also has the capacity to detect changes in the burrow's temperature, as sensed through its skin.

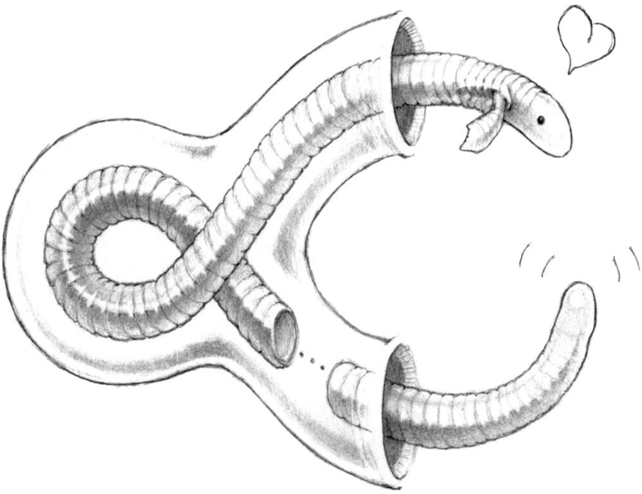

"A mole lizard can detach its tail when pursued by snakes or other predators, in a manner that plugs the tunnel long enough to allow the ajolote to flee forward."

This fossorial reptile has come upon a rather remarkable adaptation to living in narrow tunnels. It has developed a curious means of blocking its tunnels so that potential predators cannot reach it. A mole lizard can detach its tail when pursued by snakes or other predators, in a manner that plugs the tunnel long enough to allow the *ajolote* to flee forward, then take refuge before the predator can clear away the blockage in the burrow. Of course, losing its tail is a profound sacrifice that limits its locomotive agility for a while, but it is far less costly than losing its life.

To be sure, it has taken a Herculean effort by herpetologists to learn even this much about such cryptic reptiles, because five-toed mole lizards spend more than 95 percent of their time below ground. For years it was assumed that their kingdom of tunnels was restricted to the sandy plains and gravelly arroyos of central and southern Baja California, but then, in 2009, Royce Ballinger spotted one along San Carlos Bay on the Sonoran coast of the Sea of Cortés. (Surely it didn't tunnel under the sea from Baja to Sonora, but could it have rafted across with the flotsam carried by flooding following a hurricane?)

It is humbling to realize how little we know about when and where they get around. One herpetologist, T. J. Papenfuss, spent thousands of hours in the field following stray leads to locate and study five-toed mole lizards. Of the 2,719 live mole lizards he encountered, only three were found above ground in broad daylight. When I have frequented some of that same terrain—the sandy flats around a half-dozen desert oases between San Ignacio and Todos Santos on the peninsula—my meager efforts to find signs of them have been fully fruitless. Although I prowled around dozens of burrow entrances within their range, the ones I investigated were more likely used by kangaroo rats and rattlesnakes than by mole lizards.

Of course many of our kind can humbly concede that the lives of most other species on this planet are hidden from us, beneath our feet in the soils and seas, or beneath our skin in our ears, mouth, stomach, guts, and other unmentionable cavities and crevices in our bodies.

Should we ever happen to get a fleeting glance at any of these cryptic representatives of subterranean, submarine, or subcuticular biodiversity, it would be by accident. And the glass we view them through is no longer a handheld magnifying glass; it is either an electron microscope, a high-resolution bathyscope, or hyperspectral imaging scope, fluorescence imaging instrument, photoacoustic microscope, or laser speckle contrast imagery camera. By their very nature, these high-powered instruments distort or disturb the difference in scale between "us" and "them."

Even if we incidentally or randomly encounter such organisms as mole lizards in earthen tunnels, or others in oceanic caverns or human intestines, we often fear them simply because we are unable to shed much light on their lives, so dissimilar to our own.

Perhaps that is the context in which the seven-inch, five-toed, two-legged, blind-eyed mole lizard has become mythic, dreaded by many of its neighbors in Baja California, for it tunnels around in the ground beneath their feet where the desert sun never shines. If only one in a thousand mole lizards ever rises above ground to be seen with our own eyes, the rest of them dwell in some liminal place in our collective subconscious beyond our comfort zone.

They survive and thrive deep in the desert sands, much like the giant sandworms in Frank Herbert's classic *Dune* trilogy, making our skin crawl whenever they surface. But even when they remain below ground, they incite an entire range of fears and anxieties that psychiatrists have classified as chronic phobias: achluophobia (fear of darkness), anginophobia (fear of chest pain, suffocation, or choking), antlophobia (fear of being caught in floods), bathophobia (fear of the depths), claustrophobia (fear of closed or narrow spaces), scotophobia (fear of dark or dimly lit spaces), stenophobia (fear of narrow spaces), and taphephobia (fear of being buried alive).

If we suffer from any of these phobias, we have little empathy for a creature that lives where we dare not go. It prefers a subterranean world where any mole lizard must constantly repair tunnel walls of sand that are always caving in, where snakes may chase it, and where vision no longer works as a means to perceive danger or sanctuary. Instead, it absorbs and "tunes in" to vibrations below our bandwidth of hearing, and tracks scents so subtle that the human olfactory system hardly ever cues into their significance.

Hence, five-toed lizards are called *fossorial* species, with physical, sensory, and physiological traits that enable them to burrow, claw, dig, and dwell in tunnels where most humans would be petrified with fright. It is curious that it is often called in the driest of lands *ajolote*, a Hispanicized term derived from an ancient term in Nahuatl dialects that means "water slave" or "wet servant."

My friend Lee Grismer—the premier herpetologist of Baja California—has aptly put it this way:

> In my experience, no reptile strikes more fear in the hearts of local inhabitants than this *ajolote*. Almost anyone [in southern Baja California] . . . will tell you that its suppository-shaped head facilitates its penetration into the human anus. . . . Its long claws grip the walls of the rectum and serve to anchor it in the intestinal tract. The short limbs are used to locomote deeper into the body.

As Grismer grimly detailed the Californios' fears of this intruder, he added, "even when you simply ask the locals if *ajolotes* live nearby, they instantly slap both hands over their butts as if to protect themselves from these mole lizards!"

Another herpetologist, Carl Franklin, has claimed that should you need to drop your trousers and squat when nature calls you on a camping trip in Baja California, an *ajolote* may enter your body through "unspeakable means" as it rips through your guts, tattering them to bits as if they had been grated through a paper shredder!

While there are no confirmed cases of the act, there persists a local legend in Baja that the Mexican mole lizard will climb up into an unsuspecting bathroom-goer's most private orifices.

Dan Sharp, a UK-based researcher of animal behavior, has noted on his Fact Animal website that "this local myth has given the Mexican mole lizard a bad reputation that can sometimes be fatal should a particularly squeamish person find one minding its own business near a bathroom."

To set the record straight, several desert reptiles are feared by Indigenous and rural women of arid lands, but not because they ever enter bathrooms or lurk in toilets. In the era before outhouses and other kinds of privies proliferated in desert communities, both women and men often "went" outside—sometimes behind a woodpile or downwind of a sandy hummock with bushy mesquites or acacias that offered protective cover. Unfortunately, these are exactly the kind of microsites where five-toed mole lizards and other fossorial reptiles come up for air.

We might speculate that the "fear of penetration" by a lizard was justified among desert dwellers in bygone eras, and that reasonable fear extended to possible intrusion into several of the nine or so orifices of the human body. Pulling down petticoats and skirts or bulky pants behind a stack of firewood or a bunch of live branches did indeed have its risks, simply because lizards love hiding in woodpiles, windbreaks, living fencerows, or natural patches of desert trees with limbs akimbo. This fear of penetration into one or more of the human orifices by any lizard may seem preposterous to an urban dweller back East, but when I have listened to elderly women who grew up in rather rustic conditions out West, they bluntly admitted that dancing with lizards was no laughing matter. Even if a mole lizard only climbed up the hem of a skirt, the crouching individual suddenly jumped up faster than a coiled snake prank toy exploding out of a cylinder of Pringles potato chips.

And so, the disturbingly tragicomic consequence of having mole lizards as your desert neighbors in bygone days is that they not only tunneled into the ground beneath one's feet, but they also came to hide in seldom-traveled passageways in the human psyche. We might even postulate that *ajolotes* became "encrypted" in the collective unconscious of desert dwellers over decades, centuries, or millennia of infrequent interaction.

And yet the mythmaking in Mexico about *ajolotes* is richer and perhaps stranger than that. This Mexican name used for mole lizards in Baja California is derived from folklore about another creature on the Mexican mainland that is not a reptile but an amphibian. The

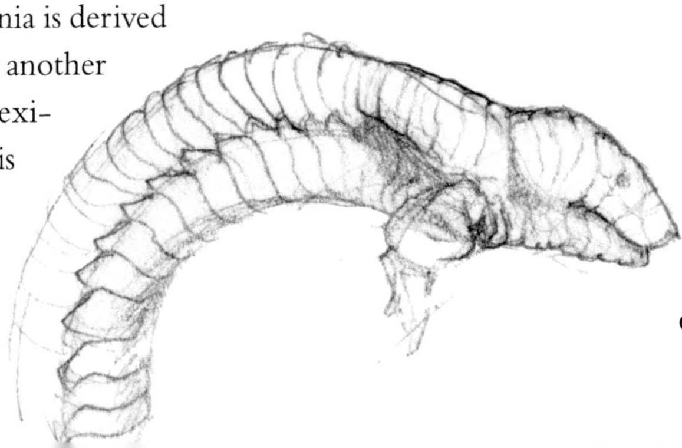

Californios of central Baja likened some traits of their lizards to those of altogether unrelated salamanders found in central Mexico. There, *axolotes*, scientifically known as *Ambystoma mexicanum*, are mucus-covered salamanders with external gills, endemic to the wetlands of Lago Xochimilco just south of Mexico City. There are in indeed "water servants."

Their name comes from the Nahuatl term *Axolotl*, which was also the name of the ancient Aztec god of fire and lightning. Their ability to drop their limbs and then regenerate them made them a symbol of reincarnation and renewal. According to creation narratives first recorded in the Nahuatl language, there was a moment when all deities were forced to sacrifice themselves for the birth of the Fifth Sun. At that moment, Xolotl, the twin of Quetzalcóatl (the plumed serpent), mutated into the water monster now known as *Axolotl* to halt the sacrifice of so many embodied spirits.

As *Axolotl* was transformed into a salamander-like water monster, he dove into the Lago Xochimilco, where he remains to this day. Ironically, the remnants of Lago Xochimilco have been partially drained, degraded, and dirtied by decades of urban development and tourist attractions, but they survive as the last functioning semi-intact wetland habitats of the endangered, endemic *axolote* salamander.

When and how the apparition of this salamander-like creature in Mexican folklore ended up more than 3,200 miles north of a small lake in the Valley of Mexico—to dwell as a mole lizard in the deserts of Baja California—is just as mysterious as its leap over to the desert coast of Sonora. All this is a tangible reminder that the flotsam and jetsam of animal folklore have floated up or tunneled down into places far from their point of origin. For some, they have delved deeply into the orifices of both body and mind, to eventually dwell where most of us do not want any intruder to go!

GREATER ROADRUNNER

The first morning I moved into my new home in Patagonia, Arizona, I was greeted by a greater roadrunner on the front patio, who pumped his tail up and down three times before dropping a housewarming gift of bird poop on the Saltillo tiles. It then sprinted away so fast that it seemed to vanish before my eyes. I did not know then what I know now: that my first houseguest was the largest cuckoo in North America, and that it would be returning to visit many more times over the next few years, leaving other presents at my door: snakeskins, scorpions, lizard tails, and tarantulas. Each time it arrived for a brief visit, it seemed so sleek and muscular when it was approaching, but when I got a closer view of this roadrunner, it appeared disheveled and homely, with so many feathers in disarray that I was a bit shocked. It reminded me of a hobo who had just walked out of a Salvation Army thrift store with used clothes that did not match or fit his body. But it did not have to look pretty in its kind of work; it merely had to be a delivery bird on the run from place to place. The first published linguist of the Tohono O'odham language, Juan Dolores, once conjectured that the greater roadrunner's role in life was to carry news back and forth across the desert. And that he did: from 1949

to 1973, the Road Runner cartoon character teamed up with Wile E. Coyote to give people all around the world some of their first views of desert landscapes on film and television. While many viewers in the United States, Mexico, Albania, Hungary, Indonesia, and the Philippines may have assumed that the Coyote and Road Runner sagas were completely made up from scratch, the originators of these Warner Brothers cartoons filmed in Disney Studios riffed off the writings of Mark Twain in *Roughing It* and folklorist J. Frank Dobie's writings in *The Voice of the Coyote* and *The Roadrunner in Fact and Folklore*. Dobie had recounted many Native American and Hispanic folktales of coyote and greater roadrunners, in which these somewhat cunning, wacky, and audacious characters bear the brunt of their own excesses and presumptions through a variety of hilarious misadventures. The first cartoon with these two critters together was a six-minute skit released in 1940 by Looney Tunes and Merrie Melodies called "Fast and Furry-ous." The great voice of cartoons of that era, Mel Blanc, did the vocals for Wile E. Coyote, while Paul Julian came up with the car-horn "beep-beeps" that became the only words ever said by the Road Runner over two decades of their adventures together. If you had to decide whether to travel for a day with the greater roadrunner or Wile E. Coyote, which would you choose?

CHUPACABRA

Beginning with a mysterious massacre of Puerto Rico goats more than thirty years ago, the specter of a cryptic goat-sucking creature that leaves no marks, blood, or survivors has spread like a shot heard round the world to scare the *mierda* out of one Latinx culture after another. Although agrarian communities in the Caribbean and the Americas faced horrific *matanzas* of the livestock long before the first report of chupacabras on the loose, it seems that the sudden emergence of goatsuckers in the popular press and media weirdly fit like hand-in-glove with the rising tides of mass deaths of human victims nearby, suggesting a ruse at the hands of dictators, mafiosos, paramilitary squads, and thugs, many of whom love to make headlines in lurid tabloids as much as chupacabras do. But what terror they generated as campesinos responded by gassing and torching hundreds of caves, where they guessed that chupacabras might roost, killing thousands of innocent bats and birds from Utah's canyons to the tide-splashed grottos of Sinaloa. When law enforcers dispatched fifty armed cops and fifteen vets to a Sinaloan farm where goat-sucking monsters had allegedly struck the night before, the only suspect they could find in the farmyard that night was a feral dog, and the next night, another dog with mange, with so little fur left on its back that they could see scaly, diseased skin. When a wildlife pathologist investigated twenty-two other incidents much like this one, the only plausible cause he could offer was that the goats were attacked by feral hounds, junkyard dogs, or coyote infected by scabies, a microbial pathogen, *Sarcoptes scabiei,* which had killed the goats before the curs themselves were killed. And so no matter how many chupacabras appear on T-shirts, posters, billboards, Vimeos, and YouTube postings, there is nothing new about these sickly predators. Might we say that they simply signal the unsettling feelings we have for monstrous afflictions that have always been among us, around us, and in us, which flare up from time to time as palpable expressions of the vague notion we imprecisely call *evil,* as if naming it might be enough to vanquish them?

SEVEN

REGAL HORNED LIZARD

War Monger or Pacifist?

Sometimes, I am so puzzled by English common names for animals, for I can't figure out why they hardly ever seem to reflect the essential character of the beast they refer to. That the desert creature scientifically known as *Phrynosoma solare* throughout the U.S. Southwest is called the regal horned lizard has baffled me for a long time.

It is bad enough that *Phrynosoma* is derived from Greek terms that imply toady-looking bodies, given that most of them are rather svelte and streamlined. Sure, their protruding bellies may drag on the ground, but that is because their stomachs need 60 percent more space to hold food and moisture through extended droughts than most other lizards require. But their bellies never bulge as much as those of any of the true toads on the face of this earth.

Dense ironwood is heavy but will burn long and hot.

It would be regarded as rather offensive and insulting if humans called any of their own royalty or family members "toady," although there have most certainly been English kings and queens over the centuries who fit that description well. At the very least, that descriptor fits the British aristocracy better than it fits any horned lizard.

I know I may come across as being a little overly sensitive about this issue; the taxonomists are simply pointing out that *Phrynosoma solare* is the only lizard in its genus with a "crown" of flattened horns clustered near the back of its head. But that alone does not give the lizards a "regal" appearance any more than a barrel cactus with a ring of thorns around its head looks particularly royal.

From what I know of these lizards' demeanor from my fifty years of frequent contact with them, they are humble, gentle, and often unobtrusive—all traits that we seldom use to describe a duke or duchess, queen or king, emperor or empress. And yet I was relieved to learn from the writing of my Yoeme friend Felipe Molina that his kin regard the regal horned lizard's "crown" to be reminiscent of that of the Virgin of Guadalupe. For that reason, *pahk'ola* dancers seek the help of this lizard they call Santo Mochokol. What a relief to learn that horned lizards or "Ant Eaters" were being revered like saints rather than like kings or queens in a militaristic monarchy.

Nevertheless, I prefer the common name my Comcaac friends use for horned lizards. In their language, Cmique Iitom, they call it *hant coáaxoj*, with *hant* meaning "earth, soil, earthlike," and "in or of the earth"; and with *coáaxoj* meaning "opening, entrance, or place within." It is related to the term *coáaxyat*, "the place where the spirits of the dead lay."

This is a bit of speculation, but we might say that the Comcaac regard horned lizards as "spirits nestled into the earth," or alternatively, as "cryptic spirits resembling the open ground or the earth itself." The crypticity alluded to by this moniker comes from camouflaging themselves with the same mottled colors of the earth below them, while assuming the most flattened, humble posture possible. These

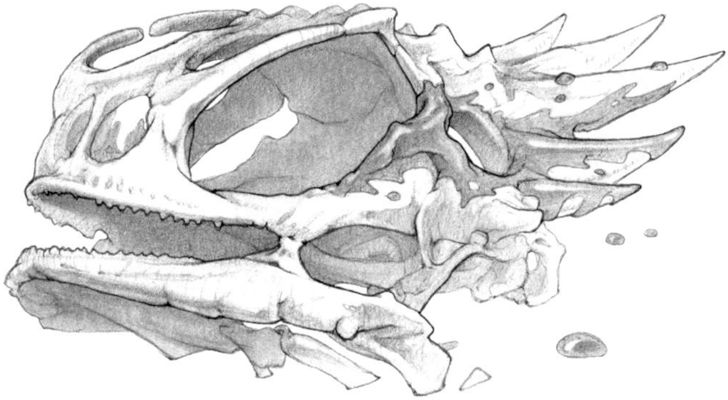

"[T]he muscles around the lizard's sinuses contract in a manner that ruptures them, ejecting a stream of blood that can be propelled as far as five feet from its body."

two factors are often enough to keep many potential predators from spotting them. Sometimes they even roll over "dead" or fade into the background rather than having to choose between fight or flight.

Horned lizards do occasionally employ another line of defense that has made them infamous among the masses: *blood squirting*. While some desert dwellers assume this blood-squirting defense mechanism is a bunch of malarkey, horned lizards do resort to this defensive behavior one in twenty times when they are provoked by humans. Still, they largely employ this tactic against canids, who find the fragrance and taste of their toxic liquid so distressing.

The renowned Wade Sherbrooke sat me down one day to explain to me what his team had learned about how and why horned lizards squirt blood. Squirting out toxic blood plasma from the sinuses around their eyes is all about deterrence. When alarmed, the muscles around the lizard's sinuses contract in a manner that ruptures them, ejecting a stream of blood that can be propelled as far as five feet from its body.

Amazingly, Wade discovered that the source of the toxin and stink in their blood plasma comes from their most common prey items, harvester ants in the genus *Pogonomyrmex*. "*Pogos*" themselves are among the most aggressive and venomous animals on earth, up there with tarantula hawk wasps. So when they bite a potential predator, it suffers from one of the most lethal stings known, due to at least four potent enzymatic compounds in the ant venom: phospholipase, hyaluronidase, acid phosphatase, and lipase.

Curiously, horned lizards eat dozens of *Pogos* a day without harm, consuming high doses of toxins that can irritate the esophagus or stomach of any other lizard. But the toxic enzymes found in *Pogo* ant venom are metabolized and muted in most horned lizards by the mucus-secreting papillae (bumps) in their mouths and on their tongues. When enough of the irritant compounds from their ant diets are sequestered into their own circulating bloodstreams, it enhances the antipredator utility of their blood squirting. In addition, any predators who happen to bite into a horned lizard from behind may get a particularly high dose of these toxic compounds from the lizard's blood, high enough to make them foam at the mouth, shake, or flee. The unsavory memory of this traumatic moment helps to reduce the chances they will ever assault a horned lizard again!

Wade convinced me that the squirted "blood" is exclusively reserved for pugnacious dogs, cats, bobcats, coyote, foxes, and the rare, ridiculously aggressive human, not other species with which they coexist. Even though horned lizards may compete with other animals for food, water, or space, blood squirting is never mobilized as a defense against snakes like diamondback rattlers or coachwhips, roadrunners, or leopard lizards, or even the grasshopper mice that often tangle with pinacate beetles. With most of their animal neighbors, they maintain docile live-and-let-live behaviors.

Some observers have suggested that horned lizards simply cannot be understood in any dualistic "either/or" manner. They report that a horned lizard may simultaneously project a ferocity *and* a down-to-earth humility. A few scientists regard them as timid, but others assert they can display a combative countenance reminiscent of carnivorous dinosaurs and the fierce monsters of the imaginary kind we cringe at when we see them in B horror movies.

I am not sure I agree with that last assertion. The presence of a truly monstrous animal in your yard might break up your household, but horned lizards do not seem to be home wreckers. Even for an animal that exhibits blood squirting toward potential predators like coyote and dogs, it is a defense mechanism, not a mode of attack per se. Unlike *Pogo* venom, the squirted-blood-laden fluid startles rather than injures its assailant.

It may be a stretch to portray horned lizards as aggressive, simply because they sporadically employ this one defense mechanism. In fact, they have several strategies for avoiding conflicts. As my late great friend Rafe Sagarin explored, we would do well to pay more attention to the range of strategies horned lizards use to deter or repel rather than kill or injure their enemies, because they might metaphorically help our country's security strategists find better solutions to avoid rather than engage in conflict.

This exercise might help us fend off terrorist attacks, bomb threats, mass shootings, and disruptive strategies like "swatting"—sending fake calls to emergency numbers to distract tactical units from mobilizing to deal with real threats to the public. But which specific horned lizard behaviors should our military and homeland security experts try to comprehend and mimic in their own peacekeeping campaigns?

They roll over and "play dead" to feign inactivity or illness to avoid conflict.

They use geomimicry and biomimicry to camouflage themselves to evade conflicts, with pigments in the scales changing hues to match the mix of background colors of pebbles and leaves on the ground. Against red and brown gravel, the horned lizard's brown and red pigments allow it to blend in with the colors in their background, while the jagged shapes of their horns create broken outlines that blend in with the texture of their substrate. On a gray or sandy-tan background, horned lizard pigments also shift their dominant hues to better blend in.

They employ "Batesian" mimicry through squirting low doses of smelly enzymes derived from the ant venom that echoes the olfactory warning signals developed by more toxic harvester ants to deter predators.

They use their horns—which they employ less for jousting and more for collecting, channeling, and depositing reserves of rainwater for later drinking—to appear more dangerous than they are, visually bluffing and blustering predators into thinking that they will suffer potential harm by attacking them. Nonetheless, their cranial horns—the ones that give them their so-called regal appearance—do indeed give pause to their predators. If these cranial horns are clipped, there is a higher level of predation on horned lizards. But once they are swallowed whole, horned lizards have one last defense that may or may not kill their predators—as both the Diné (Navajo) and Comcaac (Seri) confirm in their traditional stories: *swallowed* horned lizards can indeed cut their way through the stomach lining, integument, and scales of a snake, and explode out into freedom!

I, too, have witnessed rattlesnakes and coachwhips that died after swallowing a regal horned lizard, for the thorns on its head pushed through their respiratory passages and protruded from their skin to the degree that the predator expired. But I see more glory than gore in this last-minute move by the lizard to live a bit longer. I would liken it to the Hail Mary pass that my favorite quarterback—Roger Staubach—threw to Drew Pearson in the last seconds of a Cowboys-Vikings game in 1975, cinching a shot at the Super Bowl for an all-rookie team.

The wonderful Comcaac woodcarver, the late José Luis Blanco, once crafted for me an ironwood carving of a horned lizard cutting its way out of a sidewinder. To my surprise, José Luis chuckled, then charged me twice the normal price of a reptile carving, arguing that

it was an ingenious two-for-one representation. It was an offer I couldn't refuse! I also watched the grandchildren of José Luis over many years, who acted with love, not trepidation, while caring for the regal horned lizards that lived around or in their village of Punta Chueca, Sonora. Horned lizards had become their favorite pets! In fact, I once saw Jose Luis's three granddaughters, all between the ages of five and eight, walking past their grandfather's house one morning for school, carrying shoe boxes with horned lizards lounging in a few inches of beach sand.

When the girls reached the edge of their village, each of them found an anthill on which to place her pet, or *mascota*, so it could eat its breakfast before school began. When the first warning bell announced that classes were to begin in ten minutes, each girl affectionately picked up her breakfast guest, put it back in its shoebox, sealed the lid on the box so there would be no chance of escape, and placed the box back under her bed where the lizard rested until after school was out that afternoon.

The caring stewardship and tenderness that each of these children displayed for their wild pets were quite touching. I had never read of terms of endearment for any other wild pet that included a requisite of providing two meals a day of fresh ants.

While many recognize the gentle, almost timid conduct of these lizards, others feel from them an unflagging charisma, a sense of composure, confidence, and dignity. It is hard to write those feelings off as being purely anthropomorphic. Some, like my friend Mona Polacca, a Hopi-Havasupai-Tewa elder, looked to them for guidance when she was a little girl, growing up in the canyons of Arizona:

> I would see horned lizards on the path in front of me, as if alerting me that the trail was safe to travel. It was [as] if they were saying, "These are your relatives here ahead of you, and you are on the right path."

Of course not everyone believes that their role models—human or otherwise—can simultaneously express humility and undaunted charisma under challenging conditions. For my part, I never worry about being poked by horned lizards' sharp-edged horns as if they might blind my eye or turn lethal, and I have never heard of a human who has died at the hand of a horned lizard.

In the Comcaac Indigenous communities where I have been blessed by decades of friendship, the mere suggestion that ants or other animals may sting one of their beloved horned lizards to death is agonizingly nightmarish. And yet it is featured in a cautionary tale that reminds every Comcaac child to watch out for and avert this peril through the loving behavior of *being good allies*. They simply never wish to see any horned lizard injured by ants, coyote, or dogs, or taunted and tortured by reckless humans. Causing harm to *Phrynosoma solare* is strictly taboo and enforced not only among the Comcaac themselves but also for any visitor, construction worker, off-road vehicle driver, or road grader who comes into their villages.

I learned about the depth of their protection for horned lizards only after having the name Hant Coáaxoj bestowed on me by Comcaac families over two decades ago. Virtually everyone in both Comcaac villages knows me by that name; in fact, very few children in their fishing villages know me by any other name. They now say that the name was initially given to me honorifically because a single individual was amused by some traits they felt I shared with their affable friend. But instead, it was really given to me as a joke of sorts, for the first song I ever sang in their Cmique Iitom language was about a horned lizard, and it took me long hours to memorize the fleetingly short nursery rhyme.

Because it took me two months of constant coaching by elders to get my pronunciation of every word in the song rendered correctly—while it often takes less than a day for one of their infants to master the same rhyme—they granted me the provisional use of that name as a reminder that my song-learning capabilities were more "infantile" than those of their infants! Or as one old man bluntly put it, "Hant Coáaxoj, you have less of a singing voice than that little animal does, and you are more cluelessly vulnerable in the desert than it is, so that's why we have decided to protect you from perils just as we protect it!"

Well that prognostication should have gone a long way toward making me as timid as a horned lizard, but it didn't. Instead I immediately asked them to teach me the longer story that explains the riddle-like nursery rhyme about the cryptic horny toad, which made them roll their eyes and groan. But many of them valiantly offered their own versions of the parable, many of which I recorded by memory or notebook, whichever I had on hand that day.

After years of hearing perhaps twenty renditions of the story behind the song—all varying from one another in one or more key details—I have given up on believing that the Comcaac have anything equivalent to a single official "King James" version of this story, which has been granted a consensus of opinion by tribal elders. And so I will offer you a pastiche of key features associated with this parable. I sense that a decentralized, nonauthoritarian, heterogeneous aggregation of 1,200 people might not even care if there is not a single "authentic" or "true" version of this horned lizard fable that has survived over time immemorial, that is, since the era when a horned lizard was a sentient being in their community that could talk with others as easily as you and I might converse today.

The core story was recounted to me by Isabel Torres, who was already blind by that time. When I greeted her, she turned toward my voice. I sat down in the sand on the shoreline and held her hand, then sang her the *Hant Coáaxoj Coicos*, the cautionary tale for children about a horned lizard who was once part of the Comcaac community:

> You haven't been told, have you? That Horned Lizard, the one you sang of in the song, well, he was a person. You thought all the time that you were merely singing about a little animal, didn't you? Well, it was a long time ago [that it happened], but this Horned Lizard man on Isla Tiburón went looking for firewood for his people [who were cold and hungry]. But he didn't come back alive.

He had gone out in service to the others who were either too weak or too lazy to get firewood to bring back into camp. So he went it alone, going up into the mountains, slowly piling firewood up on his back to carry back to the camp on the shoreline where everyone else had stayed. As his burden became heavier, he trudged more slowly back toward the village until he was so tired that he fell flat against the earth. He was nearly buried under all the wood, pinned against the ground.

"The ants?" I asked, having heard that ants may have contributed to his demise. "The ants killed him?"

"Yes, the ants . . . The kind that the horned lizards eat."

A swarm of ants stung, then dismembered and ate the one who typically ate them.

"Ahh," I began to understand. When he didn't return by nightfall, the others in the camp could have immediately gone out to rescue him, but they didn't. When they finally went searching for him, he was just a horned cadaver. "And so, they found only his remains and the firewood."

The firewood he had labored to bring back to them to save *their* lives.

Señora Torres nodded.

"They knew it was him by his bones. That happened long ago, of course, in a time when that man was known by the same name as that humble little animal. I just wanted you to know, because we've given that name both to you and to one of the boys in the village. You share that very same name: Hant Coáaxoj."

She let go of my hand and began to chuckle. "So, all this time you must have thought that we were only singing about animals!"

Later when I was with her peer, Ramón Perales, I asked him if he also knew that Hant Coáaxoj had been a walking, talking, firewood-hauling individual deserving of personhood.

"Of course! He was a Man before the last world was destroyed, and this world was created. He died when he went out to get firewood for the rest of our people back when times were hard. They later found just his bones. But his life went on, and when this new world was created, this Man's life came into this humble, little creature."

"The man . . . from those ancient times? Do you mean . . . how do you say it? He was reincarnated? His spirit . . . it's in the animal?"

Ramón nodded. "Yes, Hant Coáaxoj. What you would call his *soul*. . . . Who knows? Maybe it is in you, too. That's what one of us may have recognized in you when she gave you that name!"

How humbling it is to be called a Horned Lizard when I know that old friends like Ramón Perales and Wade Sherbrooke have delved far deeper into the soul of Hant Coáaxoj than I have ever glimpsed.

CRESTED CARACARA

The crested caracara appears to be the most elegant scavenger of roadkill and offal the world has ever known. And yet a case of mistaken identity plagues us: the mythical caracara is neither eagle nor vulture. Eagles they are not, for they belong in the same family with falcons and kestrels. As the true national bird of Mexico, this stunning specter is sometimes conflated with the golden eagle, a bird poorly portrayed on the Mexican flag, and the bald eagle, the national bird of the United States. In some Indigenous and Spanish dialects, caracaras are called yellow-headed vultures, for they sometimes scavenge alongside, or compete with, black vultures and turkey vultures. But their lineage is far removed from that of vultures, even though they ecologically share eating habits with these other scavengers, seldom killing prey but dining on carcasses and entrails left from butchering. One dawn on the Feast of Saint Francis in Topawa, Arizona, I observed crested caracaras gathering with the two true vultures around a ceremonial ground. It was where Tohono O'odham elders were preparing to butcher a steer, cutting it into cubes for red chile con carne to be offered sacramentally that night to festivalgoers. After the steer was hung high between two posts and blessed by both a traditional *makai* (medicine man) and a Franciscan priest, its entrails were removed and placed on its hide. The hide was then pulled by five strong men forty yards away from the center of the ceremonial grounds. It was left as a "first fruits" gift for all the caracaras and vultures gathered there for the ceremony, who swept down from the tops of tall saguaro cacti to devour the tripe, blood, and other offal. In Sonora, crested caracaras are sometimes called *queleles*, a name commonly used further south in Mexico for its more

tropical kin, or *quebrantahuesos*, or "bone-breakers." My Tohono O'odham friends call these faithful residents of their homeland *kúusijim*. When watching one crested caracara along with me and Amadeo Rea, O'odham elder Delores Lewis laughed at the way that it slicked its shiny black head feathers back to look like pachucos from the zoot suit era in Los Angeles and Mexico City. It is curious that Delores associated them with pachucos, because crested caracaras are historically associated with events that occurred between the city of Pachuca, Hidalgo, and Mexico City, just sixty miles to the south. In Nahuatl religious beliefs in central Mexico, both caracaras and hummingbirds were associated with Huitzilopochtli, the deity of the sun and of war. He is the one who ordered the Aztecs to abandon Atzlán, their mythic place of origin in the north, to search for a more productive area further south, where their Mexican civilization could flourish. Huitzilopochtli told them to look for a sign that informed them where the heart of their enemy, Copil, had been thrown into a lake after he was slain. The signal they recognized was Huitzilopochtli's caracara perched atop a cactus, eating a serpent. That particular place in the Valley of Mexico, southwest of Pachuca, would become known as Mexihco Tenochtitlan, an island in Lago Texcoco, and later simply as Mexico City. As the lake was drained to reduce flooding in the city, part of the dry lake bed became one of the world's largest landfills, accumulating more than 70 million tons of food waste and trash piled more than fifty feet deep. Was that some kind of payback to the crested caracara, so that it would have enough to scavenge through for the rest of eternity?

CONDOR

They remain the largest land birds in North America, with weights of up to twenty-five pounds and wingspans reaching nearly ten feet from their heads. We still call them California condors, as if statehood has something to do with their natural range. It does not. The last populations of desert condors stayed in the wilds of the San Pedro Mártir massif in Baja California. Some flew out across the Sonoran Desert. Others kept to the Sierra Madre Occidental and Grand Canyon. The Baja Californios should get credit for keeping them alive until government recovery teams emerged; lead, rampant development, and fire suppression in Alta California are what endangered the species. Baja was the source of those used in the captive breeding of birds whose five hundred or so descendants are now found in Alta California, Arizona, and Utah. But oral histories also document them in the foothills of the Sierra Madre on the Sonora-Chihuahua border, and in the Midriff Islands of the Gulf of California. There is more to their story than that. When I once took my Comcaac mentor from Sonora, Alfredo Lopez Blanco, to central Baja California with me, I was browsing the pages of a book on the rock art of the peninsula when he stopped to show us a group of animals he had seen painted in one of the caves we visited in the Sierra de San Francisco. "Look at them more closely," he suggested, "I believe they are condors." "Condors?" I asked, baffled, "How do you know condors?" because they disappeared from most of the peninsula and from Sonora by the 1920s. "Well, my family saw them on Isla Tiburón in the 1930s, way up near the most rugged peaks on the island. They were so big and different from vultures, we discussed those encounters many times." But perhaps the deepest traditional knowledge of desert condors comes from the Hopi, who knew them from centuries of contact in the Grand Canyon, where they called them *kwaatoko*. Even today, conservation biologists deem the Grand Canyon "the best place to reestablish the beleaguered condor" because they are relatively free there from the risks of lead poisoning, poaching, and intrusive developments. Where I lived for eight years between the Grand Canyon and the Mogollon Rim, reintroduced condors and Mexican gray wolves may have occasionally fed on the same carrion. The times I've seen condors soaring alongside me out from the rim of the canyon or diving toward prey below me have been among the most terrific moments I have experienced in the desert Southwest. Seeing two or three condors fly within twenty yards of me made me wonder: was it the size of this scavenger that struck me with awe? Or was it the fact that humans had brought such a bird nearly to the brink of extinction that made me feel so awful?

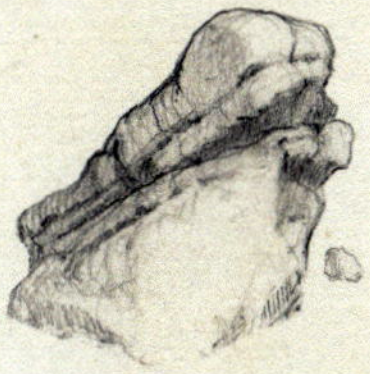

EIGHT

LA CORUA

Water Serpent—Protector of Springs

For years—even decades—I had heard of snakes protecting springs but without ever seeing such "water serpents" that guard these sacred upwellings. They protect other vulnerable sources of water too. My imagination was ignited, and my eyes grew wide every time I heard of "protector reptiles," that is, water serpents set to safeguard any water body to ensure lives survive there. According to my Opata friend, Cristina Murrieta, these serpents dwell in grottos, caverns, and crevices where they can guard *nacimientos de agua*, a profoundly poetic term for the birthplace of artesian springs.

Many of those springs are linked to cultural origin narratives of desert peoples, acknowledging them as spirited sources of health and well-being. Even wild animals show deference to them. These protective spirits go by various names, but their mythic roots may be the same: La Corua (Sonoran Spanish), Quetzalcóatl (Nahuatl),

Stone-still sits a living seep.

Kurues or Corúa (Yaqui or Yoeme), Coruba or Baco (Opata), Ñee-ibig (Tohono O'odham), and Coimaj Caacoj (Comcaac).

I could see them slithering along in my mind's eye, glistening and glimmering like rainbows as they arched themselves over fallen branches above the water's edge. I could hear their rustling and hisses echoing off the canyon walls above the springs, and I could smell their dank odor as they arose from the murky, tannin-rich waters and mud.

At the same time, I had been rigorously trained by field biologists who maintained what they called "a healthy skepticism" that such creatures had ever existed in the flesh. They regarded the stories about such reptiles as nothing more than apocryphal, fanciful "fables" simply meant to scare the living *bejeebers* out of indolent teenagers.

As I hung out with some technically adept biological scientists over the years, I gradually came to realize that some of them had let their healthy skepticism slide into a nasty cynicism about such "folklore," generating a disdain for agrarian people who saw value in keeping such stories alive in their cultures. For some of these zoologists—but thankfully not all of them—the domains of "myth," "legend," and "oral history" are fraught with factual errors, fallacies, presumptions, and wishful thinking. They posit that human memory is frail and that human imagination "makes monsters appear" where they have not been borne out by scientific fact.

At the same time, I experienced moments when bright, caring, finely educated individuals from several different desert cultures would say things to me that gave me pause. On a trip to see Hopi springs of the edge of Black Mesa, Arizona, my friend Vernon Masayesva changed our plans on a moment's notice simply because we were arriving at an unfortunate hour to be at a culturally esteemed dwelling place for such potent serpents. It happened one autumn day when we had fishtailed our way down a sandy road to arrive below a sacred spring that had offered irrigation to Hopi agricultural terraces for centuries:

"Oh, it's just *not* the right time to be here . . . It is best that we don't go any nearer to the place I thought I might let you glimpse. But we aren't prepared, we don't have the necessary permission or guides, so frankly it would be dangerous to go any further. This is a spring protected by the water serpent *Paaloloqangw*. . . . Who for us is something like a deity for water . . . one we shouldn't mess with."

And so we erred on the side of discretion and turned around before I got to see the spring that was hidden up on the mesa edge above us. I later learned that *Paaloloqangw* once emerged on the wet surface of a Hopi plaza, where it then drowned nearly everyone who hadn't fled. Vernon knew far more about such incidents than he bothered to tell me that day, but I was grateful for his restraint.

And yet at that same time, I could hear the voice of one of my scientist mentors sitting on my shoulder, whispering in my ear, "What is there to be afraid of? There might not be any snake at all by those springs."

A chance occurrence changed my way of thinking about such matters a few months after that visit to Black Mesa. My wife, Laurie Monti, and I were riding horses not far from the desert coast of the Sea of Cortés north of Guaymas, heading inland toward Cañon del Nacapule, a subtropical oasis of wild figs, palms, and hundreds of other lifeforms. We were being guided through the Sierra del Aguaje by José Antonio "Delfino" Magayán, who ran a small livery stable and knew the canyons there like the fingers on his own hand.

On some spontaneous whim as we loped along, I simply asked Delfino if he had ever seen a *corua* in those parts, since there were so many small springs in that slickrock landscape. As he turned in the saddle to answer me, he caught some movement out of the corner of his eye and shouted, "Look, there is one now!"

I turned in the direction he was pointing just in time to see a five-foot-long boa constrictor—the serpent he knew as *la corua*—slither up a tree and swallow whole a *cenzontle* (mockingbird) that had been perching on the uppermost branch. In another second, it had disappeared into the dense underbrush below the *guamúchil, bebelama*, *mezquite*, and *palo fierro* trees alongside our riding trail. Delfino paused along the trail, stunned as much as I was. He noted that he occasionally spotted them lingering in mottled shade above the *aguaje* seeps and *tinaja* kiss tanks fed by the springs in that sierra. According to Delfino, they sit and hypnotize the birds that they will soon prey upon.

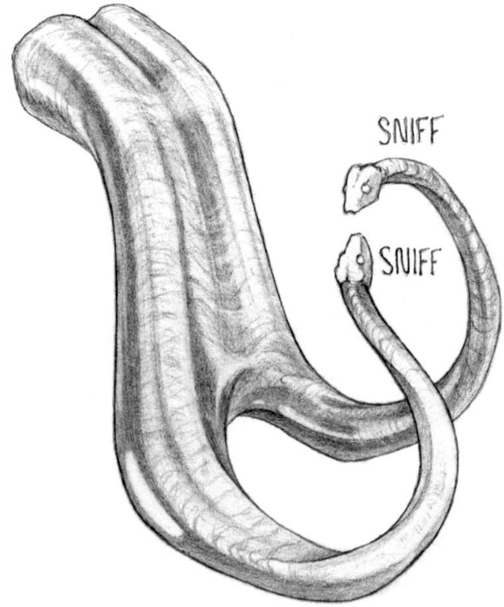

A forked tongue allows serpents to take in two scent samples at once. When two samples are registered and compared in the roof of the mouth, the direction of a smell can be determined, much like our depth perception that comes from having two eyes working in stereo.

Those coastal *coruas* were not all that far from their boa species' present northernmost limits along the Sea of Cortés coast, but they still reached further north some ways inland, within a hundred miles of the U.S.-Mexico border. But who knows what their geographic limits were prehistorically, when many cultures that now live in the desert were still migrating around the subtropical savannas, montane forests, and desert seas? Today we fleetingly catch a glimpse of the cryptic *coruas* in just a few watered sites over thousands of square miles. But where else might water-loving boas have lived in the past, when springs were a hundred times more abundant in the days before groundwater pumping, poor grazing practices, and climate change slayed more than four out of five artesian springs that once bubbled up on this planet?

Ancient place names may help discern where those former springs occurred. Their northern limits are likely to have shifted over the last few centuries. In palm oases found in canyons in the Río Sonora watershed, their historic presence is commemorated by the Opata Indian place name Bacoatzi, not far from the former Sonoran capital of Arizpe. It is derived from their terms *ba* for "water," *co* or *coa* for "serpent," and *tzi* or *tzic* for "place of."

The pueblo currently called Bacoachi (Bacoatzi) is less than seventy miles as the serpent slithers from the present-day U.S.-Mexico border. But Bacoatzi and Arizpe are situated along one of the most significant cultural trade corridors in the desert region, reaching as far north as the Hopi, Tewa, and Zuni pueblos in the Four Corners region. Stories of boa constrictors no doubt spread northward from Mesoamerica with itinerant *pochteca* traders from the Aztec Empire, or with spiritual pilgrims who used the Río Sonora as a pathway for their sacred journeys. They would carry the tales, not the skins, of boa constrictors with them to seed the imaginations of their hosts in the north.

When the Spanish first came through the Bacoatzi-Arizpe stretch of the river, Pima or Opata were living in mesa-top pueblos of multistory, aggregated dwellings much like those still found in the Hopi pueblos that edge Black Mesa. The languages of both the Hopi and the Opata are in the Uto-Aztecan linguistic family that also maintained *cóatl* as the name for water serpents farther south in Mexico, where the plumed serpent Quetzalcóatl was revered.

We might back up for a moment; we must ask why some snakes and serpents are revered in one set of cultures, but found to be repugnant as phallic symbols or reviled as predatory, often poisonous monsters in others?

First, let's acknowledge how physically impressive these memorable snakes appear. Keep in mind that boa constrictors of the species *Boa imperator* are the longest and thickest nonvenomous snakes found in the deserts of North America. They generate awe, but not as much fear as the venomous rattlesnakes, coral snakes, and fer-de-lance do in these or other parts of the Americas. All that is to say, boa constrictors are terrific but not always terrible or terrifying, for they lounge around the edges of springs as if presiding over them or protecting them.

And what could be more important to a desert people than to have a formidable guardian of one of their scarcest and most sacred resources—artesian freshwater springs that are usually the last source of potable water to be desiccated during droughts, wildfires, or warfare?

I have heard from several Comcaac elders that there is a serpent called *coimaj caacoj* in a water hole near the summits of Isla Tiburón; this serpent does not let anyone drink there, except with its permission. When all the other *aguajes* have dried up during droughts, it remains as the last potable water in a parched land. Once, they say, when a Mexican cowboy on horseback climbed up to those heights and wanted to water his horse there, he heard hissing. Then he glanced down around the water's edge and saw the scorched and seared fur of deer left in piles, as if it had been burnt and blown off wildlife that had not bothered to ask the guardian serpent for permission. The frightened cowboy did a quick about-face and fled to seek safer water elsewhere.

Where the Hia Ced O'odham once lived along the Sonoran coast, I have heard from them the tragic story of a Spanish brigade of mounted cavalrymen and missionaries that arrived at a large *tinaja* or tank in the Sierra Pinacate. To the horror of the Indigenous desert dwellers, the soldiers and their horses quickly "liquidated" hundreds of gallons of freshwater that the migratory "sand people" could have survived on for months.

Not only did the military force some of Hia Ced O'odham to flee, but the Ñeeibig, the legendary water guardian serpent of O'odham tradition, may have also moved farther inland, or deeper back into caves, where neither the water nor its protector can now be revealed. For decades, there have been few serpents left standing to offer enough protection to keep springs and waterholes from being desiccated or defiled with horse manure. But in its heyday, the Ñeeibig would appear near a desert oasis and draw intruders toward it, sucking them off their feet as it inhaled, then digesting their flesh and spitting out their bones as a warning to others.

Such stories of diasporas by humans and imaginary menageries are seared into the hearts and souls of desert dwellers around the world, as I've learned from my own relatives who live by spring-fed wetlands on the Lebanon-Syria border. My relatives lament the drying up of springs near Kfar Zabad, Lebanon, as much as the Hia Ced O'odham do in Arizona and Sonora. Protection from disrespectful outsiders may be one reason that serpents like *la corua* are said to have the symbol of a cross engraved above their eyes. Mess with it, and you are messing with a spiritual force.

The Comcaac traditions regarding Coimaj Caacoj are outside the Uto-Aztecan language family and are full of curiosities I am at a loss to fully explain. There are some similarities to other Sonoran lore but anomalies as well.

We are not aware of any boa constrictors that ever swam out to Isla Tiburón and survived there, so some families refer to the coachwhips or *chicoteras* in the snake genus *Masticophis* as the gigantic *coimaj caacoj* of that desert island. But Comcaac fishermen know there is another marine reptile named *coimaj caacoj* in the sea channel between Islas San Esteban and Tiburón. It warns them that passage to San Esteban is risky for those who do not know how to appease the water serpent there.

There is a deep geological fault line and canyon-like crevasse between the two islands, which creates roiling eddies and sea swales so high that you often cannot see over the waves before you. Our friends claim that the sea serpent guards the straits and lashes his tail out at any travelers who show disrespect, smashing their boats by swishing their tails.

Cleotilde Morales Colosio of Punta Chueca worked with my wife, Laurie, to record for her descendants a navigational song cycle of the Comcaac in which appeasing and calming Coimaj Caacoj is a key dramatic element. Eight to twelve songs are sung by the women to guide their husbands, brothers, and sons through the treacherous wave field, fraught with rolling tides and eddies. When we hear the stacatto rhythms over the tumultuous waters there, a calm comes over the navigator and the passengers, so that all can remain alert, staying wary of any upcoming perils during the journey.

In ways, the songs are akin to Australian Aboriginal songlines, which assure safe passage across the desert by reminding pilgrims to focus on each upcoming challenge or crossroads. The memorable, trancelike songs sung by Comcaac women keep Coimaj Caacoj as an ally, rather than letting him rage as an adversary.

We know of no other culture in the greater Sonoran Desert region that keeps a respectful relationship with both a serpent of the seas and a frequenter of freshwater springs. But in both habitats, they are simultaneously protectors of preciously scarce resources and beasts who may go on a rampage at a moment's notice if riled.

Water serpents like *la corua* and *coimaj caacoj* simply can't be pegged as good or evil, and plugged into pat, dualistic categories. They are both protectors and predators. They can be creatures of turbulent waters and underwater caverns out at sea, or cryptic characters that conceal themselves, climbing high into the dense vegetation that forms rings around desert springs. They can be both voracious ambush predators and diligent sit-and-wait fasters who demonstrate patient perseverance. They may evoke the fear that macho males emit, or the warm embrace of a maternal figure in her lair. They leave us with dread and wonder.

Not one of us can adequately describe all the dimensions of these water serpents, because they simultaneously attract and repulse most of us. Those of us who have been fortunate enough to catch sight of their agility and stealth for a few moments carry that haunting image with us, subconsciously and consciously, for decades. They remain a paradox that neither science nor faith can fully circumscribe, so we wallow in fear or tingle with awe even during the briefest of encounters. They inhabit our dreams as wildly as any creature, reminding us of the slippery realities found in parched lands and effervescent waters. They take us back to primordial places, where the bitter aridity of deserts interdigitates with hypersaline seas or sweet underground aquifers.

But these guardians of freshwater springs may remind us that we all need to guard what is left of these rare aquatic ecosystems. Nine out of ten historically recorded artesian springs have already been lost in desert landscapes. Because of the significance of the remaining springs to both endangered species and cultural traditions, we all need to be engaged in safeguarding these fonts of diversity.

CRAWFORD'S GRAY DESERT SHREW

For such a long name, this meek creature is minuscule, hardly ever reaching two inches or weighing in at above five grams. The only time I glimpsed one—for I was not intentionally looking for a shrew but examining the razor-sharp leaves of a sotol or desert spoon—it leapt off the old leaf debris at the base of the trunk and then disappeared in a millisecond. It is reputed to be the smallest of all mammals in the desert Southwest, and desert shrew babies emerge when they are barely the size of honeybees. Globally, "Crawford's Gray" is ranked among the humblest of all homeothermic mammals in the world, sustaining a very narrow range of body temperatures internally despite all the extremes of heat and cold that others may suffer in the high desert habitat they share. To achieve such resilience in the face of so many climatic stresses, it has become "hyper," racing through its caloric reserves at such a rapid pace that its tiny heart must beat about a thousand times per minute, or ten times faster than the most "hyper" human. Prone to hyperventilation, this homely soul huffs and puffs eight hundred times per minute to suck in enough fresh air and pees out urine four times as concentrated as any that human beings

spill onto the earth. If that were not enough to scare away most dates, it spends most of its time in the dark, so it must constantly make high-pitched, shrill squeaks to navigate by echolocation just as many bats do. Its more winning traits are its fine sensitivity to sound and scent, thanks to its talented ears and long snout. As far as preferences for bedding down, desert shrews are not very picky regarding where they lay their heads, agreeing to sleep in brush piles, fallen trees, or hollows in the short trunks of yuccas, sotol, and prickly cacti. They have been known to occupy abandoned packrat nests as well, but never, ever do they dig a new burrow. While there is no evidence that they have sought to be listed on dating websites, they have a knack for finding partners willing to keep their *raza* alive and kicking. Is this what a desert prophet meant when he preached, "Blessed are the small in spirit, for theirs is the kin-dom of heaven?"

NINE

EL CARBUNCO

Bump and Shine Beast

When any elderly dweller of deserts, barrancas, or sierras tells me about a rare animal that I've never seen, I make sure I remember as much of his or her description as possible, on the remote chance of a later encounter with such an animal. There must be some vault in my memory bank where a hidden menagerie rests, waiting for me to meet its members in the flesh.

My mentor, Howard Scott Gentry, once told me how, in the 1930s, he had heard of the strange nocturnal animal that campesinos called *el carbunco*. While Howard had worked as a paleontologist, wildlife hunter, and plant explorer in the Río Mayo of Sonora during the Great Depression, he lived among Guarijio and Mayo Indian farmers, treasure hunters, prospectors, and herdsmen in San Bernardo, Sonora. In the mid-1970s, Howard introduced me to Juan Arguelles, a native son of the barrancas surrounding San Bernardo,

Like a lizard's pineal eye, sharing the light it once captured.

who had guided Howard on mule trips into the Sierra Madre. Juan had this to say about this elusive critter:

"The *carbunco* is a small, haired animal, slightly smaller than a house cat, which carries a light in its forehead. There are very few, and they come forth from their ground lairs only at night. The light they carry is presumably to enable them to see their prey. It is like a blue stone and emits a bright white light. They are very wild and will run if one approaches, and they will immediately extinguish the light which betrays them, so one is unable to follow them. They live in rocks just beyond Chorijoa, where a few have been known to come forth in *las aguas* [the summer monsoon season]."

And yet, after Juan spoke with us, I remember being intrigued that Howard found this account by Juan to be incredulous, even though he clearly admired Juan's protracted attention to wildlife. When Dr. Gentry wrote up a narrative of his field explorations in southern Sonora and Chihuahua from 1934 to 1938, he called Juan's account of *el carbunco* "a myth." Howard admitted that commentaries by local residents like this that filled his field journals from the Sierras were either his own "direct observations and of what I heard and learned. It is therefore partly hearsay, so, to reduce errors to a minimum, I have checked one source against another, a method which, with time and patience, leads to verify . . . believing that I would snare more truth and less falsehood."

Given that statement, it is curious that Howard included any mention of *carbunco* in his very first scientific publication, which he wrote in Mexico. Oddly, his account was not edited and published until thirty years after he first put pen to paper in his field journals from the 1930s. As a young man, Howard was both a subsistence hunter and an astute observer of wildlife in the outback of the Mother Mountains; he did not miss seeing much of the fauna or flora of northwest Mexico during his decades of exploring its more remote regions. He spent years on foot or mule in the Sierra Madre Occidental, on the plains and in the barrancas of Durango, all along the Baja California peninsula, and in many parts of Arizona and California. But to think that some mammal or reptile undetected by science could still be "out there," waiting to be discovered and scientifically described during his era, was a possibility that fascinated him, as it does me.

Within two years of Howard's death in 1993 at the age of eighty-nine, I felt compelled to do something to fill the void left by his passing. I organized a grassroots effort to identify where and what long-time Sonoran residents had seen when they referred to *el carbunco*. At the "Celebration of Desert Cultures" events in Caborca, Sonora, in 1995, I offered over two hundred dollars in cash as prizes to those who offered the best two or three accounts of *el carbunco* as seen in particular places. Friends from many *rancherías* helped me put up posters all over Sonora to attract those who claimed to have witnessed the animal.

But just as the contest was about to begin, folklorist Big Jim Griffith pulled me aside at a café to alert me to something I had overlooked. He looked at me sternly, which immediately caught my attention, due to the fact that Jim usually clowned around with me.

"Gary, you are acting as though the *carbunco* has had just a recent presence only in northwest Mexico, but it is actually ancient and widespread! The ancient Greeks knew of a shining stone that grew under the fur on the heads of unicorns. It was ruby-like and in some cases, could heal wounds. And an animal with carbuncles on its forehead was described in medieval Spain and France; some say it has a brilliant light that emerged from an ugly mass of bumps or knots above its eyes. *El carbunco* may be far more ubiquitous and well-known beyond Sonora and Chihuahua than what your posters imply!"

I was floored. But when I got back home and dug into library collections, it became clear that Big Jim was right (as usual). He had fortunately kept me from assuming that *el carbunco* was just a provincial phenomenon in the local yokel lore of northwest Mexico, for that had indeed been what both Dr. Gentry and I had presumed.

Nonetheless, both Big Jim and I were delighted when Sonorans of every ethnicity and walk of life arrived to take part in our little contest. *El carbunco* was still very much alive in Sonoran parlance, as novelist J. P. S. Brown, my neighbor in Patagonia, also confirmed. Up on a ridge above the Río Mulatos, Joe Brown had once seen "a bright orange flash of light like the flare of a match," in a place where both Indigenous and mestizo goldminers identified such sightings as the nocturnal movements of *carbuncos*. His Sonoran hosts told him that the sightings of *carbuncos* were often associated with hearing bells ring where there were no homes nor churches. They were ominous warnings, an old vaquero confided in him.

Dozens of contestants—from age eighteen to eighty—told us tales in Caborca, grassroots stories that were delightfully akin to those that Juan and Joe had offered me. Several contestants simply noted that *carbuncos* always appear near hidden treasures of precious stones. Others said that *el carbunco* appeared as a foretelling of one or more deaths soon to occur. They offered us index cards highlighting the salient features and intriguing behaviors of *el carbunco*, hoping they would be selected as finalists for our storytelling panel.

We whittled the contestants down to just three sets who seemed the most promising based on the index card highlights we had solicited, but the most intriguing card was submitted by three railroad workers. They had worked together on the track line between Benjamin Hill, Sonora, and Mexicali, Baja California Norte, from 1937 through the 1990s. They claimed to have mapped the distribution of known sites where *carbuncos* had been seen over hundreds of miles in northwestern Mexico. This group was among the three finalists we selected.

The first contestant was an elderly man who remembered seeing the light from the head of *el carbunco* fifty years earlier, not far from Trincheras, Sonora. He confessed he could not see the animal itself, only its brilliant light, which caused the horses and dogs in the rancheria where he lived to get restless. Coyote heard the dogs barking and joined in the chorus. Then *el carbunco* vanished from sight.

Good start, but not much detail.

The next man lived in Caborca where he had developed a flair for play-acting tall tales in the most humorous fashion. He told of how, when he was young, his father was a hunting guide for Americans who came to hunt bighorn sheep and mule deer in the arid ranges near the coast. His father would get the Americans drunk on mezcal and then tell them to wait on an elevated deck until a strange glow appeared in the desert, and that it would be *el carbunco*, a rare game that could be made into a fine trophy by taxidermists.

When the gringos were both tipsy and tired of waiting, the boy would turn on a flashlight that his father had fastened onto the head of a mongrel dog and let it loose so that the hunters could see it run and fire at it in the dark. The trouble was that the gringo sportsmen were such bad marksmen that the boy nearly got shot by them, while the frightened dog bolted from the scene, dropping his flashlight as he scurried away. The crowd we had attracted howled with laughter, becoming more convinced every minute that *el carbunco* was just a hoax featured in a Sonoran version of snipe hunts.

But when the railroad workers came on stage, these *ferrocarrileros* looked rather indignant that anyone might think *el carbunco* was only a prank. With much pomp and circumstance, two of the men ceremoniously unrolled a scroll with their hand-drawn map of the natural range of *carbuncos* on it, while the third caballero took out a pointer that he waved around with flourish to direct our eyes to key points of interest on the map. All three of the men were dressed in their best double-woven Sonoran palm sombreros, crisply ironed snap-button Western-style shirts, polyester pants, and Yuma cowboy boots.

The map was a blueprint blow-up of the Ferrocarril Sonora-Baja California railroad line from Benjamín Hill to Mexicali. On it, they had posted inch-diameter red dots to broadly indicate where they had made a sighting of *carbuncos*. Each dot spanned five miles.

As I huddled with the contest judges, they wanted to know more about the dots on the map. So I courteously asked the caballeros in my most flowery Sonoran Spanish subjunctives for more detail.

"Well, we only saw them during the night shift, while we were working on trains headed west. The trains would stop at various water tanks along the line [to] re-water, and if one of us spotted a solitary light—or three or four out in the distance—we would count that as a sighting. Of course, since it was dark, we seldom caught a good view of the animal itself."

"But what was their preferred habitat?" I asked.

"Habitat? What do you mean? Where they have dens? We don't know," the oldest man confessed. "But where exactly they roam along the railroad tracks for roadkill is what we do know. We saw their lights just off the steep banks of the raised bed ahead of us on the railroad tracks. We always spotted the lights from their heads out maybe a hundred yards or so from where we were on the tracks. They were probably frequenting the fresh carcasses, old mine shafts, or the water holes that the railroad line was built to connect."

"But if there were no tracks in that terrain, do you think they would still be there?"

"Hell, we don't know, we're just humble railroad workers—brakemen, switchmen, and gandy dancers—not *mastazoológos* of wildlife. But if we win your contest, maybe we would have enough gas money to see if they ever lived farther away from the tracks!"

With that, the crowd assembled for the contest started to laugh and shout, "*Los ferrocarrileros ganaron! Los carrileros ganaron!*"

It was a perfect closure to a contest with a flawed design, since the term *ferrocarrileros* meant "railroad workers" or "trackmen," but *carrileros* alone was a nickname for "tricksters."

The threesome went home with a one-hundred-dollar grand prize to split among themselves, while each of the other two contestants garnered fifty dollars. The trick was on me. Everyone seemed happy.

Back at the library after the "Celebration of Desert Cultures," I found the historic references that Big Jim had alluded to. There were *carbuncos* in Europe described in the *Etymologiae* attributed to Isidore of Seville in the early seventeenth century. Subsequent scholars noted that the terms *carbunco* and *carbunclo* are derived from the Latin *carbunculus*, which originally referred to something or someone glowing like red-hot coals or shining like rubies. Other historians have suggested that *el carbunco* is akin to an animal known as *guivre*, which had a precious gemstone embedded in its head, serving as the guardian of mines of precious minerals. It seemed that the name *carbunco* described a mammal with a third eye that shimmered like embers, and this eye was surrounded by carbuncles—bumpy skin or clumps of blisters suggesting dermatological irritation or infection. That ring of blistered skin was ominously called "the halo of death."

In the first recorded instance in the New World, Gonzalo Fernández Oviedo y Valdés reported finding *carbuncos* between 1512 and 1526 near Santo Domingo, in the present-day Dominican Republic. But rather than writing it off as a questionable "myth" as Gentry did four centuries later, Oviedo y Valdés grouped it with five other animals that zoologists now believe went extinct in the West Indies over the intervening years. Fossils of at least one of these rarities have since been found, but the others—*coris*, *hutias*, *mohuys*, and *kwamis*—remain unexplained. Oviedo y Valdés—a trained scientist—did not believe they were merely fabrications from sloppy, uneducated observers. They were palpable, observable beings that lived in the era when Europeans and their livestock first intruded upon the New World.

At first, as I read these accounts of *carbuncos* that had been recorded over four centuries, it seemed as though they were describing several different mammals that shared only two characteristics: a third eye that flashed light in the darkness, and a cluster of carbuncles that surrounded it. I began exploring two possibilities to explain the diverse range of animals that shared this name. My first guess was that the shape, size, color, and character of imaginary *carbuncos* continued to "evolve" or "morph" into new forms as stories of this animal and its activities were transmitted from medieval Europe to reach more remote areas, Argentina, Chile, the Dominican Republic, Haiti, Mexico,

"In South America, the spread of carbunco traits came to reside in an animal akin to armadillos, with a hard shell covering the top half of its body . . . The entire animal folds up and closes so tightly that it looks like a dull stone or clamshell."

Paraguay, and the Philippines. But in most of these tales, they had bumpy skin and an odd light emanating from their being.

The other possibility was that, after the introduction of livestock to the New World, a wide range of mammals began to suffer from a cutaneous infection that had already been known in the Old World for some time. The infectious disease generated horrific changes in the afflicted fauna, including bumpy, blistery skin on their foreheads, blisters that broke out into wounds that glistened with orangish or ruby-red blood, or skin that gleamed or glimmered with bluish or lime-green pus. The behaviors of afflicted animals changed as well, making them leap into the air and run around wildly at night in a manner different than most animals of their kind.

In South America, the spread of *carbunco* traits came to reside in an animal akin to armadillos, with a hard shell covering the top half of its body; in Mexico, they appeared in midsized mammals like coatimundis, skunks, racoons, and ring-tailed cats; elsewhere, they were observed in cryptical creatures that may have been moles, weasels, or small wild felines like margays and jaguarundis. Some of these wildlife species were omnivores, others were carnivores.

A few observers alleged that *carbuncos* developed a heightened sense of hearing that served them well at night, when they would bound around erratically, as if bewitched or burdened by extreme nerve pain. Some campesinos claimed that before the *carbuncos* vanished from sight, their entire bodies were cast with a burning glow, as if they were succumbing to a high fever or internal combustion. The "halo of death" seemed to fit with these descriptions.

But just as I thought I was getting close to an explanation, I was overwhelmed by a flash flood of distractions. There was a rash of new expressions involving the term *carbunco* that began to make their way into pop culture. Perhaps the interest in this creature was rekindled by the Nobel Prize–winning author Jorge Luis Borges, who included *el carbunco* in his 1957 literary romp, the *Manual de Zoología Fantástica* (Handbook of Fantastic Zoology). The book became so popular that, as it was translated into several other languages, he and his co-conspirator, Margarita Guerrero, kept adding "species" to it, including 116 in the English translation released in 1969. It became a cult classic among hippies in Europe and the United States, who already indulged in trippy sword and sorcery fantasies. *The Guardian* called it "a map of the endless labyrinth of human imagination."

More recently, the postmodern *carbunco* has become somewhat of a cyborg, appearing in Pokémon, Dungeons & Dragons tabletop games, Pathfinder's Age of Lost Omens, and the Final Fantasy role-playing video game series curated by Hironobu Sakaguchi. These allusions made it abundantly clear that *el carbunco* had not yet become culturally or biologically extinct, as the *coris*, *hutias*, *mohuys*, and *kwamis* have over the last four hundred years.

Its "third" eye has never disappeared either. It has been persistently seen, although some twenty-first-century observers now claim that it has become a mirror set into an eye socket where a third eye might otherwise reside. *A mirror?* Is *el carbunco* simply a reflection of ourselves? If not, might we relate its third eye to the vestigial "third eyes" shielded by the scales in some reptiles like mole lizards? This additional sensing organ is reputed to aid these species in setting their circadian rhythms.

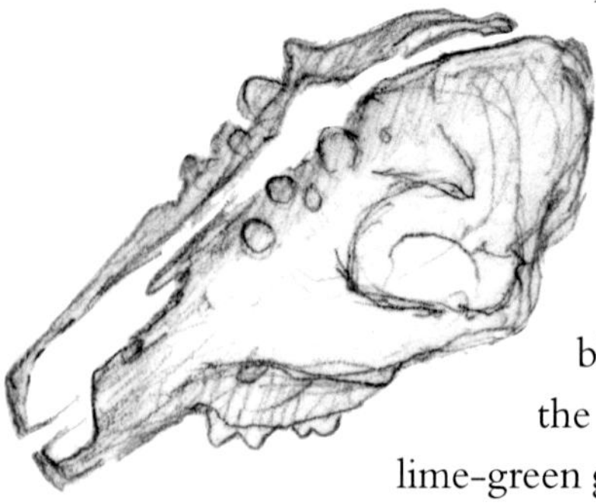

Some insist to this day that the luminosity of *el carbunco* is fiery red-orange; others observe that it emits a blue-white light, while still others claim the entire beast is shrouded in a curious lime-green glow. But when alarmed or chased, this creature is said to cover its beam with a thick, shutter-like eyelid, a furry flap, or a hood. Then the entire animal folds up and closes so tightly that it looks like a dull stone or clamshell, undetected by most passersby.

As I read on, these morphological transformations simply made less and less sense to me, and I began to lose interest in pursuing this mythic critter any longer. But what kept me in the game was a hypothesis that the bumps, or boils, or clusters of blisters on the skin of *carbuncos* might be caused by viral or bacterial infections. More recently, microbiologists have homed in on some relationship between the animal itself and the bacterium called *Bacillus anthracis* (anthrax), one that may be among the deadliest microbes to surface in certain parts of the world today.

Most physicians had no way at all to link symptoms of specific microbes to animals until Robert Koch first discovered the evil ways of the anthrax *Bacillus* in 1876, thereby ushering in the dawn of medical bacteriology. He did have some pretty adept predecessors: Louis Pasteur had homed in on the fact that bacteria caused putrefaction of the flesh, and Jacob Henle, who taught Koch human anatomy in Göttingen, championed the concept of *contagium animatum*—that some deadly microbes were being vectored by animals. But these "germ theories" made little sense to Europeans who had never peered into a microscope to witness tiny but tenacious organisms whose cycles of life and death turn around like a Ferris wheel gone out of human control.

Koch had a chance to test the theories of Pasteur and Henle when he got a job as district medical officer in Wöllstein, where he immediately had to deal with an emerging crisis that had killed over five hundred people and over fifty thousand head of livestock in less than four years. The German farmers in the countryside around him had noticed that when certain livestock pastures became havens of death for various breeds and species of livestock, they would remain so for years. Pathologists soon noticed that rod-shaped structures were readily seen through microscopes in the blood of both human and porcine victims, and that healthy rabbits, cows, and sheep could be afflicted with these structures if inoculated or exposed to spores in the blood, hides, or soil surrounding the afflicted animals.

In the lab, Koch figured out the life cycle of the bacterium that became named *Bacillus anthracis*, while his field collaborators described a cutaneous form of anthrax that infested its victims with raised, itchy bumps, then ugly clusters of hard nodules with black centers, then swelling around the sores and nearby lymph glands, accompanied by fever, headaches, and other symptoms. Depending on the European language of the pathologists in these laboratories, they would use either *anthrax*, *carbuncle*, or *carbunco* for the vernacular name of the pathogen!

The term *carbuncle* is still used by English speakers for any nodule-like bumps around a wound, but in Spanish parlance, the term *carbunco* became the most used term for the anthrax bacterium, not just for the bumps of the skin that are the first signs of infection.

And yet it appears that the use of the term *carbunco* for the deadly disease caused by the bacterium *anthracis* was not a new phenomenon, but rather echoed the spread of the industrialization of the livestock industry and its containment of high densities of animals in feedlots. It has been used for centuries to describe the disease symptoms that have frequently appeared in livestock that inadvertently fed on infected corpses, and that occasionally spread to humans. To be clear, anthrax has never been a disease that exclusively affects livestock like cattle, goats, sheep, domestic hares, and camels. It has also been found in rats, kangaroo rats, pocket mice, deer, antelope, wild rabbits, and monkeys. It inevitably and indelibly changes their appearance and behavior.

So what if the term *carbunco* was never intended by rural cultures to taxonomically identify a particular species of animals but to alert other humans to beware of *a range of animals known to be affected by anthrax* for their own protection?

Far too often, when contemporary readers peruse a historic document about animals, they take certain terms to be formal "taxonomic" names rather than fluid descriptors of the animals' health conditions, developmental stages, behaviors, or phenological expressions. But preliterate rural cultures around the world had no Linnaeus among them to "fix" a single name to a particular animal species; their use of terms was far more wily, adaptive, and pragmatic. To warn their children or neighbors about the possibility of a rare but deadly infection, adults might alert youngsters to be on the lookout for any unusual or abnormal appearance among the animals around them, because they had no idea which animal species anthrax might infect next.

And so the elders might use storytelling to seed their memories with cautionary tales that kept listeners wary of the unexpected, as unanticipated infections could kill a cluster of crawling toddlers, a colony, a clutch, or a litter lurking around the same household.

We might laugh at the maps of known *carbunco* occurrences offered by storytellers at a Sonoran Desert festival, but what if there is a seed of caution in those stories that has survival value? That may be why Howard Scott Gentry was never completely dismissive of the "myth" that our friend Juan Arguelles told about *el carbunco*. Flummoxed, yes. Healthily skeptical, yes . . . but still curious.

Nevertheless, many rural Sonoran Desert dwellers might be surprised to learn that *el carbunco* is not merely the name of one species of animal that got caught in the beams of a railroad locomotive or in the headlamp of wildlife biologists. It is a loose grouping of animals that exhibit carbuncular bumps on the skin around their eyes and glands, discoloration of their hair or fur, and bizarre shifts in their behavior. These symptoms are more attributable to the interaction between a bacterium and an infected vertebrate animal than to any distinct species of mammal, bird, or reptile.

And so *el carbunco* may be an apparition that emerges from the interstices of Gram-positive, rod-shaped bacteria and animals with open sores, from the overlapping edges of life and death on disturbed grounds in feedlots to pastures of densely packed or devastated herds, warrens, flocks, and fluffles; from the devoured flesh of rotting bodies where bacterial spores become activated; and from where our most frightening nightmares of what might be out and about in the wider world collide with microscopic killers that *are* lurking out there—beyond the tracks—every night when we close our eyes.

El carbunco may be much more than that—a reminder that we simply do not know, recognize, or categorize all the fauna that have been out and about in the lands where we have lived. There are unnamed species with poorly described behaviors and microbes lurking all around us—perhaps 7.5 to 8 million kinds of uncatalogued beings creeping, leaping, or flying around in the deserts, forests, prairies, wetlands, and streams.

And if that thought alone spooks you, so be it!

CUCUY

This hairy little monster goes by so many common names that zoologists just don't know what to do with such a shapeshifter: Bogeyman, Peppery Man, Choni, Coco, Cuca, Cucuy, or El-Cúcui. They may be synonyms for fuzzy little spirits that will scare the wits out of children when they don't go to sleep and misbehave, or kindred spirits with different traits as seen by various desert cultures. Although the first written record of a miniature monster of this ilk harkens back to a gnome with a coconut-like head on the Iberian Peninsula, by 1274 CE it had become rather fishy in appearance, and the 1457 apparition from Portugal and Spain was something akin to a tortoise. But by the seventeenth century in both Europe and Latin America, the Coco or Cucuy had evolved into the hairy terror that made children hide their heads under their covers and leap into sleep, lest something happen to them that might be entirely untasteful: *Duérmete niño, duérmete ya, que viene el Coco y te comerá*. (Roughly translated: Sleep child, sleep, or else Coco will come and devour your cells.) Some folklorists simply assume that the Cucuy was shipped across the ocean from Iberia to Latin America very early after La Conquista. I am not so sure. I have heard of the Choni of the Yoemem or Yaqui world, which shares a lot of attributes with Cocos and Cucuys, as does the ubiquitous Bogeyman and the Peppery Man. My guess

is that such ubiquitous specters crawl out from under the bed, up from basements, or down from attics whenever exhausted parents lose their cool and decide to shake, spook, or startle their restless children into shutting their eyes and mouths so they can fall asleep. Who hasn't grown up with some tiny spirit hiding until the lights go out before jumping off the bedstand, leaping onto their shoulder or into their ear, to scream, whistle, hiss, or wheeze like a little Gōlem. I particularly like the furry creature with eight limbs akimbo and the countenance of a horned lizard that first appeared around 2019 in *Los Sustos Ocultos de Frankelda,* known in the United States as *Frankelda's Book of Spooks,* a stop-action animated television series of horror and fantasy. It introduced a new generation of children to supernatural beings. Who among you can remember the first visitations you witnessed as a toddler of a shapeshifter that invaded your bedroom in such a sinister manner that you wanted to run into the master bedroom and sleep between momma and papa with your eyes cemented shut?

GILA MONSTER

One evening, after the two children in our home saw their first Gila monster, I opened the two-volume *Oxford English Dictionary,* hoping to figure out how a beaded lizard named *Heloderma suspectum* initially earned its reputation of being monstrous. What I discovered was that it was questionable whether this reptile ever fit any robust definition of a monster, but the name entered common parlance in Arizona anyway. Following the Civil War, it first found its way into print by 1873. At that time, most inhabitants of the Sonoran Desert used the Spanish term *escorpión* to refer to its spitting, a behavior that Indigenous desert dwellers also recognized but that scientists can't seem to confirm. But in those halcyon days, any critter that carried a killer toxin—in this case, one transmitted by grooved teeth—was destined to be designated *un monstro* by any Mexican vaquero or gringo buckaroo who crossed its path. Add to the horror that the reptile's teeth may clamp down on the victim's skin as the glands in its lower jaws pump venom into ripped flesh that surrounds the wounds. You can begin to see how the *habladores* in cantinas and saloons could convince any greenhorn that an exceedingly cruel monster was out waiting for them, to be tripped up or to stick their hand in the wrong crevice. And yet, deaths by Gila monster bites continue to be rare, and most historic reports of this lizard coming after a human for a killing seem to be trumped up. Curiously one of the earliest English usages of the term *monster* (written in 1556 CE) used it to describe not a reptilian or mammalian beast but a human inflicting inhuman cruelty upon other humans! The

oldest roots of our English word *monster* come from the Latin term *monstrum*, referring to an omen or warning of divine portent. And yet it could also be used to express awe about any truly marvelous being. The most widely misread behavior of Gila monsters is their tongue-flicking. As it opens its purple-gummed mouth, hissing, it flicks its forked tongue like a cobra in a horror movie, but it is simply doing what you do when you perk up your ears to listen deeply. They are participating in a most ancient and widespread means of communication in the animal world: absorbing, processing, and responding to chemical signals from their mates, progeny, foes, friends, and innocent bystanders out standing in the desert. Like many animals with backbones, Gila monsters transmit messages via sexual pheromones, which can attract mates, repel competitors, or recruit allies. But reptiles also use another set of neuroendocrine cues as a "chemical language," one that significantly influences the social and reproductive behaviors of Gila monsters. It is a cool neuropeptide called arginine vasotocin that is key to the chemosensory channels that Gila monsters tune into with a simple flick of their "tuning-forked" tongues. It allows them to selectively capture and sort volatile compounds in the air released by other animals, mostly from glands in their thighs and cloaca. Who would have guessed that Gila monsters are so sensitive that they detect and caringly retain a high density of these fragrances in their nasal cavities to then guide their decisions on whether to become engaged in courtship and mating, in territorial battles, or in flight whenever they might lose a fight?

TEN

AVES ALUZADORES

Birds That Glow in the Dark

I was out in the open desert as I had been so many times, taking a long evening walk under a full moon, relaxing as the air began to cool and move down slope after a hot summer day. That's when I first observed with my own two eyes how certain desert animals can glow in the dark. I later learned that, as humans, we may be among the few mammals who don't regularly recognize this wonder. Alas, it took me many years more—over four decades, in fact—to understand why this lapse into "anthropocentric blindness" might occur.

In the years that I sauntered out into the desert while staying in Covered Wells, Arizona, I would park my car back from the highway and wander down a long dirt road edging a dry wash. It had a scattering of cottonwoods around an old windmill that I could hear spinning and creaking in a light breeze.

On the other side of the arroyo, there was an old floodwater field that hadn't been planted for years. And yet on the last night

Silent wings and hollow, rolling trills thicken the air.

I would ever walk there, I saw a surprising number of wildflowers pushing up through the sandy loam and flood-washed debris of the arroyo. I noticed that the ground there was riddled with burrows of kangaroo rats and other nocturnal rodents. There were also some bleached-out ground squirrel bones, suggesting it was good hunting ground for predatory birds.

As I turned to leave the dirt road and walked over to see the scatter of bones over there, I spotted what looked like a small campfire ahead of me.

Oddly, it was smack dab in the middle of the road!

That piqued my curiosity, so I stayed on my course down the road rather than exploring the arroyo and the field. But that's when I realized that there was something odd about the firelight forty yards ahead of me. It looked like it had a salmon-red flame, but there was no smoke rising from it. In addition, there were no tracks of cars or trucks, nor any campers that I could see ahead of me. There was no obvious human presence at all—even recent footprints—in front of me on the road.

As I paused there, dumbfounded, I heard something glide right over my head, moving in the direction of the campfire. But as I glanced upward, I could not make out whether it was in the shape of a bird or a bat. It was more like a fast-moving glow with bursts of lightning-like sparks, like the static electricity that rises from an old wool sweater now and then.

The lights were orangish, flickering, and swooping. Or better, they were salmon-colored, like the flesh of a Chinook or Coho, but so fleeting that I did not trust my eyes.

The phantom had landed a few feet away from what had appeared as a campfire in the middle of the road. Suddenly, both specters of flame-like flashes disappeared altogether. As they vanished, I heard a metallic screech ahead of me, and then two shadowy forms veered off toward the cottonwoods.

They instantly disappeared from my sight as I stood there amazed.

I felt the hair on my neck stand up. I mumbled to myself, "What in tarnation was that?" A shiver slid down my spine.

What were those flying, glowing, sparkling forms? Bats, banshees, owls, night hawks, flying saucers, or ghosts?

Whatever they were, they creeped me out.

Without a second's hesitation, I scurried back to my pickup truck, got in it, and spun it around without veering off the road. I shifted gears and went fishtailing down the desert road below Giho Do'ag (Burden Basket Mountain). From its flanks, I sped all the way to the center of the O'odham village of Covered Wells, and into the older part of the settlement that Mexicans called Quijotoa. I parked in front of the Sacred Heart mission there, turned off the headlights, and sat there for two more minutes, trying to catch my breath before going inside.

When I turned on the light in the bunkhouse where I was staying at the old mission quarters, I saw that no one else was there for the evening. I realized I was not only dripping with sweat, but my heart was still beating loud enough for me to muffle the silence of the desert.

What in the heck had I witnessed? It took me months to remember that two of my old friends and mentors had casually mentioned to me something that might have been akin to my own vision. It took many more years to link those three spectacles into a cohesive story. That's because the identities and causes that they proposed to explain these nocturnal sightings did not seem to be compatible with what I had observed. For years, I presumed that they were speaking of very different phenomena.

When I was first living in the Sonoran Desert, a teacher of mine named Amadeo Rea was puzzling over the identity of an owl that O'odham elders had described to him many times. He could identify all the other owls that they mentioned, but not this one. But elder after elder insisted that there was one kind of owl that he was missing, even though each of their descriptions of it seemed different. Amadeo would read his notes to me, somewhat humbled but also exasperated that the clues did not fit together very well.

One Akimel O'odham elder that we both greatly admired, Joseph Giff of Laveen, Arizona, had told Amadeo that the bird had two names in his Pima language: *thondam chukud* and *memhedam chukud*. The first meant "shining owl," or "the owl that glows in the dark." The second meant that it "glides while flying." But Amadeo had also recorded a third name or descriptive term for it, one referring to its manner of flying low above the ground. Three names, one owl?

"It has a reddish glow," said Joe, "like a torch." He and other men who had worked night shifts near the Gila River had seen the light get very bright, enough to illuminate all the bushes that the flyer passed over. But then the light might get smaller, the size of a lit cigarette sitting in an ashtray. Or it might disappear altogether.

Another Pima-speaking elder whose storytelling talents Amadeo and I loved—Sylvester Matthias—wasn't so sure that just one kind of owl was responsible for the "glow" that his people know. He said that it could be any owl that carried a strange light at night, down where cottonwoods lined the Gila River:

"It is hard to see, it must be gray. It will make a light when it flies over you, you see it like lightning, quick, then it drops in front of you, running, won't fly."

"Anyway," Sylvester sighed, "It's not really a bird . . . it's halfway to being a ghost!"

Another of Amadeo's friends, Leonard Pancott, recalled that when he traveled alone at night for his work, he would see the color of fire down the tracks in front of him.

"It moves. It moves. You see it there, then the next time, you'd see it someplace else . . . not every night. Then after seeing it, it disappears."

All these men fully knew that many in their own tribe viewed owls—especially great horned owls—as sacred beings deserving of our respect. Some regard them as the disembodied spirits, souls, or reincarnations of their ancestors. As such, they are ambiguous omens—on one hand, a presence to celebrate as an indicator of contact with their deceased loved ones, but on the other, a reminder of grief, fear, or tragedy felt during an earlier time. The great horned owl—among other owls, large and small—is treated with extreme caution, for it may infect vulnerable individuals with a "staying sickness" that only Indigenous medicine women and men can assist in curing.

"[A] great horned owl flew out of the dark recesses of a giant salt cedar tree. It tore off one of his eyelids without hurting his eye . . . A Yaqui neighbor explained to him that he had been gifted by his ancestors—to see the world in two ways."

Most O'odham and Yoemem who have spoken to me about their responses to owls are deeply reverential and deferential toward them. A friend of mine, a Mexican descendant who grew up with Yoemem neighbors, once told me that at a piñata party for his fifth birthday, a great horned owl flew out of the dark recesses of a giant salt cedar tree. It tore off one of his eyelids without hurting his eye. The next morning, as he was recovering from his fright, a Yaqui neighbor explained to him that he had been gifted by his ancestors—to see the world in two ways: as an Indigenous person through the eye without a lid, and as a Mexican through the untouched eye. That combination, she said, would help him navigate his way safely through the world.

There remained the *unsettling* notion that an owl other than those known scientifically by wildlife scientists still flew at night across the desert skies. It seemed to plague Amadeo for years as a problem he alone could not solve. By 2007, when Amadeo Rea finally published *Wings in the Desert*—his lifework on traditional Piman knowledge of the birds of the Gila River—all he could conclude after twenty years of investigation and reflection was this:

> I am not familiar with any technical report of bioluminescence with regard to owls, so I am unable to explain this phenomenon of *shining owls*. The accounts of shining owls do not seem to be associated with [gases from] marshes, so the mystery remains.

Ironically, within a decade of Amadeo penning those words, reports from laboratories all over the world would confirm that there were indeed rutilant beings—birds that glowed or glistened—in our midst. In Sonoran Spanish, they are metaphorically called *pájaros brillosos errantes* or *aves aluzadores* (lightning-like birds).

Not long after we first discussed the glowing birds, Amadeo and I were present with six other friends when historian Daniel Matson told us why he had given up his vocation as a Franciscan among the Tohono O'odham around the time of World War II. He had witnessed something out in the desert with the Tohono O'odham for which he had no scientific, spiritual, or rational explanation. It had disoriented him to the degree that it shook his faith in the Catholic teachings about divine order, which he was supposed to be imparting to the Indigenous children and adults he had been called to serve.

But after he had witnessed what he had seen with two O'odham children, there was no going back. Had they "converted" him to their worldview rather than him converting them to his Catholic beliefs?

I recall how it had happened in this manner. Dan had been serving the church in Ajo, Arizona, just west of what was then called the Papago Indian Reservation, when he received a call from an office in the Phoenix diocese. He was asked if he would take the boys from Phoenix Indian School back to where their families were camping for saguaro-fruit gathering in one of the more remote desert valleys not far from Ajo.

Dan obliged and drove the church's Model T up to Phoenix to accompany the boys back home, since it was the end of their school year. But as they left the pavement to head out along dirt tracks on the reservation, they lost sight of any other human being or permanent structure. He had learned enough O'odham, and the boys enough "School English," for them to point the way to where their parents should be harvesting cactus fruit, but he had no map or address to verify what they offered to him. As the sun moved toward the western horizon, he had seen neither hide nor hair of the campers. Dan worried that he and the boys might need to sleep in the car all night if they did not arrive before sunset.

But just as sunset passed, the Model T rose over a ridge into a hidden valley, and the boys reassured him that the camp was in sight. As they moved down to the bottomlands and up onto a rocky slope just after sundown, he saw no tents, but just a few lights that he thought to be ramadas with gas lanterns or campfires. The boys pointed to a spot on the valley slope and confirmed they were minutes away. Dan was relieved because it had suddenly become very dark all around them, and he could soon get out of the driver's seat to rest.

The next moment that Dan looked up from the steering wheel and road immediately in front of them, he was startled: the "campfires" and "lanterns" were not staying put, but "moving around" on the slope. Dozens of the lights were perched up the ridge above him, as if they were in a makeshift parking lot for an all-night fiesta. But when the boys told him to stop the car so they could walk to their family's camp to where they would sleep that night, Dan noticed that one by one, the "campfire" lights were being extinguished.

"They looked like headlights that were on one moment, then dim the next, as they had been drained of all their energy."

He turned off the Model T, and its headlights faded. He saw that all the lights above him on the ridge had already blinked out, as if they were carbide lamps in cars with only eight-volt batteries to illuminate them. But when he asked the boys how many people camping at the site had their own cars, they shook their heads.

"Nobody got cars here. That's why they wanted you and your car to bring us home."

"B-but, but, what about those lights? Weren't they headlights? Cars?"

The boys looked at each other, then shrugged.

"Oh, *those*. They are just our ancestors. Maybe settling down for the night."

He was still shaking from his disorientation when the children introduced him to their parents. They offered him some beans in a large tortilla to eat and a cup of weak coffee, which he accepted, but he then excused himself so that he could sleep. As soon as he was inside his sleeping bag, he shut his eyes, for he had felt dizzy watching the spirits weaving around on the slope above the camp. As hard as he tried, he could not figure out what he had seen, but slowly succumbed to the exhaustion of driving all day long and ending his day in some spirit-filled world.

The next morning, after the family shared more coffee, beans, and tortillas with him, he drove back through the desert to Ajo. He asked the priest and the nuns stationed there if they had ever seen anything like what he had witnessed, but they hadn't. He went on to the military base further up the road toward Phoenix and asked whether they had any kind of aerial operation or missile launch the night before. They had not. So Dan turned around, went back through Ajo, and then headed east toward Tucson, arriving just before nightfall. He called in to his superiors in the Franciscan Order and resigned from his post in the church that very night.

Once again "secular" or "civilian," Dan returned home to the Chihuahuan Desert landscape around Douglas, Arizona, but remained haunted for the rest of his life by what his time with the O'odham had revealed to him.

I am sure that Dan had told that story many times in many ways over the following fifty years, but the two times I heard parts of it from him, his face was intensely expressive, but his voice revealed a deep sense of humility. His friends would offer possible explanations to him, but he would remain quiet, rather unconvinced by the options they would offer. Big Jim Griffith believed that Dan had seen the legendary *carbuncos* that Jim and I had heard of while listening to dozens of old Sonoran *habladores* recounting their favorite *cuentos del desierto*. Dan did not agree.

But another tale—recorded by our Franciscan friend, Padre David Valenzuela Maldonado, among the Indigenous Mayo in southern Sonora—also suggests that such rutilant birds are seen so briefly and infrequently that they are conflated with another, more earthbound, all-terrain creature, the legendary *el carbunco*:

> One night, we were coming home from another village, when we saw a light up ahead on a curve in the road that seemed to be coming toward us. It had a pale look to it, almost translucent. It wasn't a lantern nor a flashlight beam. It was brilliant, but with a kind of clarity to it. At first, we all kept walking toward the direction from which the light was coming, but then we became frightened. We stopped in the middle of the road because it was getting closer and closer to us.
>
> As the light approached, it was so bright that it made our eyes so open wide that we could see that some kind of luminous bird was generating it. The bird seemed to be flying while barely moving its wings, gliding along quietly while illuminating everything in its path. It was flying so fast that we hardly had time to observe its features. Just when it approached us, it turned and disappeared into the shadows of the mesquite bosque to the side of us.
>
> That's when we lost sight of this glistening bird, except that the mountain behind the mesquite thicket seemed to light up. None of us could figure out what it was, but when we got home to our village, and spoke with some of the elders, they guessed that it might be a bird that had the capacity to glow in the dark much like the animals called *carbuncos* do whenever they appeared to us on the mountain.

While *carbuncos* do indeed emanate light in many accounts, most sightings describe these luminous terrestrial creatures as mammals or reptiles, not avian creatures in flight. Others suggested swamp gas in a valley where there are no swamps, or clandestine military training operations where explosives were accidentally detonated. Still, the details didn't fit any of these proposals very well.

Amadeo and I concluded that the owls that shone in the dark were often solitary or in pairs. But the flutter of activity that Dan

had witnessed did not match up well with an owl's behavior—he saw flocks of birds flying just above the ground.

We were still stumped. It seems that both Amadeo and I forgot about Dan's account for a while, or at least, we did not mention it to one another for several decades. Then after the turn of the millennium, several scientific accounts began to be published that helped us "crack the code" hidden in the traditional knowledge of desert peoples. They had not been pulling our legs, bluffing us, or distorting reality for fanciful tall tales. They were on to something both credible and amazing long before scientists independently confirmed what it was.

But just why did it take scientists another four decades to unpack the explanation of an uncommon natural history phenomenon already reported by many rural peoples? Was the phenomenon itself so fleeting that it had inevitably been dismissed by skeptical scientists, who then relegated it to the trash can of pseudoscience?

The breakthrough discoveries concerned the peculiar properties of a class of biochromatic pigments found in feathers and fur called porphyrins. Strangely, porphyrins are the most abundant of all biological pigments but are also so prone to "photodegradation" by daylight that they are the most ephemeral colorant in any living organism. They produce super-intense colors that we can see on the skin, feathers, or fur of just a few families of birds, toadlets, fish, flying squirrels, and hedgehogs.

During daylight hours, a few of us might see how porphyrins can impart an extremely pale, lime-green hue to the feathers of owls, nightjars, bustards, turacos, and a few other birds. But in the night hours, they emit bright pink, salmon, or pale reddish hues under ultraviolet light, for those of us who do not typically notice them.

One major discovery of bioluminescent owl feathers happened by accident in a vertebrate zoology lab over a decade ago. A wildlife biologist working with mammals walked by a table full of owl specimens with a black light in his hand and was stunned by their bioluminescence!

Upon further investigation by the scientists in that lab, they realized that porphyrins fluoresced under very specific conditions just after sunset, for they emit the light they have accrued during the day for less than twelve minutes before their sparkle and glow fade from human sight. In less than half an hour, just before sunset, the wings of long-eared, barred, barn, and great horned owls shift from pale lime or rosy hue to brilliant, sparkling reds and salmon oranges, then "fade back into the woodwork" of their habitats.

So did Dan Matson and numerous night-workers among the Akimel O'odham and Tohono O'odham in the Sonoran Desert see what may have been the fluorescent wings of an owl?

Maybe not, because biologists have now confirmed that a few other bird families have wings that may luminesce just after dusk. That extends to many nightjars, including the poorwills and nighthawks that sail and swoop low over the open spaces in deserts and semiarid grasslands beginning in the first crepuscular hour of twilight.

Of course, this phenomenon might vary in intensity on cloudy versus clear nights, with or without moonlight, so their "lights" might look yellow, orange, or even lime green.

So what were the multiple lights that Dan Matson saw decades ago, or the two flying, glimmering objects that I saw in the middle of a dirt road years after Dan's revelation, if they were not *carbuncos* as Big Jim Griffith believed them to be? My first guess is that they were porphyrin-illuminated lesser nighthawks, and my second guess is that they were common poorwills. Both frequent the same areas of open desert in the spring and summer; I have also found poorwills in winter, as biologist Edmond Jaeger first described in 1950.

My former "student" in Punta Chueca, Sonora—Comcaac ornithologist Ana Maria Morales—was the first to suggest to me that poorwills and nighthawks might be part of this story. What's more, they love to land and sit on dirt roads and open creosote flats for a while, then swoop up in flocks low over ridges, washes, and ponds to pick off nocturnal insects and moths.

My old friend Marcos Paredes has come to a similar conclusion. For years, Marcos served as a National Park Ranger and river runner, then as the federal District Ranger for 245 miles of the Rio Grande that flows along the southern boundary of Big Bend National Park. He confirmed seeing "goatsuckers"—the local handle for lesser nighthawks—emitting a glow or sparkle because he has seen them right above his hot tub in Terlingua, Texas, where the Chihuahuan Desert stretches for miles out before him.

All of this has made me wonder whether the legendary West Texas phenomenon called the Marfa Lights was triggered by someone seeing lesser nighthawks sparkle and shimmer with electrical sparks at a distance. The first recorded report of this phenomenon near Marfa was from cowpoke Robert Reed Ellison, who in 1883 saw a flickering light while he was driving livestock up through Paisano Pass. He couldn't be sure what he was seeing but wondered if it could have been the sparks from a campfire of the Apache. That pass is twenty miles east of Marfa and climbs to five thousand feet above the true desert in open semiarid grassland and oak savanna. At that late date, observations by cowboys of both Lipan Apache campfires and goatsuckers were still common sights in the Big Bend landscape, so it's anyone's call.

But what can't be denied is that "Marfa Lights" are still seen on nights when no Lipans are present, and other attempts at scientific explanation of this phenomenon just don't hold much water. Since the inclusion of Marfa Lights in *Tales of the Big Bend* in 1976, hundreds of thousands of tourists come to West Texas every year, in the hope of seeing this yellow-orange specter eight miles south of town.

When I witnessed tourists on elevated platforms at the Marfa Lights Viewing Area, some smoked a few reefers or downed a few craft beers they bought at Borderlands Brewing in Alpine, the next town over. As they got higher, their shouts of "I just saw it!" increased in frequency until everyone was too exhausted to stay awake. By then, the probability of seeing a luminescent nighthawk, poorwill, or owl had lowered, but visitors' imaginative capacities had not. Some see Marfa Lights in their dreams all night long.

I am willing to hazard that on some warm summer night in the desert grasslands near Marfa, it is possible to see a bunch of lesser nighthawks picking off insects from one of those viewing platforms. I celebrate the fact that such a possibility has brought thousands to Big Bend after they watched *Unsolved Mysteries* on television or listened to passing mention of the Marfa Lights in the Rolling Stones' song "No Spare Parts," which became the number two hit on the Billboard charts in 2011.

To be clear, my hypothesis that lesser nighthawks' sparkling personalities light up the open spaces of Big Bend on summer nights does not scientifically "explain away" the Marfa Lights phenomenon. It is bigger than the facts. I suspect that future sleuths will go far beyond what I know to bridge what some rationalists dismiss as superstition with new insights from the natural sciences. With all the new technologies for analyzing night imagery, scientists are likely to detect and identify patterns that I cannot.

All of this makes me gush with gratitude for Indigenous knowledge keepers like Sylvester Matthias, Joe Giff, Ana Maria Morales, and Leonard Pancott, who were astute observers of the desert wildlife all around them, and to Amadeo Rea, Big Jim Griffith, Dan Matson, Marcos Paredes, and David Valenzuela Maldonado for trying to make sense of a phenomenon that once seemed aberrant to

Western eyes. Instead of doubting, they *listened*, then opened their eyes, minds, and souls to the improbable.

They were rewarded for doing so. What a wondrous moment it is when we see a bird glowing in the dark—if only for a split second—shedding off sparks as it flies over or before us. The sense that life can be luminous never leaves us after that.

Poets and mystics have long spoken of the "inner light" that some human women and men carry, and that some birds and beasts may emit. But with certain birds in the desert and in open places beyond it, this is no mere metaphor, for the porphyrin pigments in their feathers allow them to sequester the light of the day and fly with it, fluorescing in the night sky just after dusk. By doing so, they cross boundaries between duskiness and illumination, and they bridge or confound our own notions of brilliance and obscurity. Flashing by us, they become omens of great portent, reminding us to be alert and attentive to what we cannot initially explain, for that may help us survive and embrace the unknowns in this world.

JACKALOPE

There was a time when nearly every historic saloon in the western deserts and plains—from Arizona and New Mexico to Wyoming and South Dakota—had the head of a horned jackalope mounted on the wall. The first one I witnessed was in Prescott, Arizona, in a desultory tavern on the far end of Whiskey Row. It was positioned just above the back bar, but when the drunks had their fill and pushed their way through the swinging doors to go out and relieve themselves below the blue desert moon, there was hardly a jackalope to be seen *out*doors. Had they largely disappeared from the desert itself, only to be captive bred or protected within the walls of taverns, brothels, and cantinas? Or was it just a hokey hoax, begun around 1932 when the Herrick brothers of Douglas, Wyoming, glued deer horns on a jackrabbit in a taxidermic sleight of hand? Well, the story is more complex and charming than that initial joking gesture, as my friend Michael Branch has demonstrated in his wonderful musing *On the Trail of the Jackalope: How a Legend Captured the World's Imagination and Helped Us Cure Cancer*. For centuries, inhabitants of the arid U.S. Southwest and northwestern Mexico have told of witnessing jackrabbits or cottontails with little bone spurs protruding from their skulls like miniature horns. Although the taxidermic tradition of wedding rabbit and deer does not extend south of the U.S. border with Mexico, horned hares have persisted among the oral histories of the Wixárika or Huichol people of the Sierra Madre Occidental and high deserts found in Nayarit, Jalisco, Zacatecas, and Durango. These oral histories may have arisen from Indigenous people having encountered rabbits infected with an unusual virus that sometimes transformed their diseased cells into tall, dark gray horns or grotesque warts. Ironically, the microbiologist who first studied this cancerous virus in cottontails and jackrabbits published his pioneering research in 1933. It was about the first time that a Herrick brothers jackalope cyborg was first mounted on the wall at the Hotel LaBonte in Wyoming's short-grass prairie country. Did fiction follow fact, or did the two strands somehow form a mythical double helix with one another?

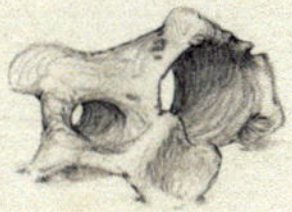

ARMADILLO

Armadillos are as common as cactus in many deserts and wear some armor as cool as that of horse cripplers and saguaro cactus to convince us they are desert worthy. Texas has the armadillo as an icon, while Arizona and Sonora have saguaros. But Texans have tried to steal "our" saguaro as a logo for their Lone Star State, where not a single saguaro naturally grows. And so, those of us in the Sonoran Desert were deeply delighted when the first few armadillos crossed the Continental Divide to head westward into the higher reaches of the Sonoran Desert, settling from Álamos (not "the Alamo") in the south to Corona de Tucson in the north. That gives us a shot at a "hostage swap," should we need one to rectify the balance between cultures on either side of the continental and cultural divide. We are filled with glee that armadillos are fleeing Texas on their own accord to take refuge in the Sonoran Desert, as they have already done in other hot landscapes of North and South America. They are settling into our habitats, homes, and yards so they do not become—as they have been from Abilene to Terlingua—little more than "hillbilly speed bumps" for Drug Store Cowboys in Cadillacs who leave a slew of road kills in their wake wherever they go—on their way to their Last Picture Show. We wish to formally welcome our new neighbors from the other side of the Great Divide by offering safe sanctuary for all of these precious but imperiled little armored vehicles with pointed snouts, bony tapered tails, and upright ears, for they have been blessed with affectionate nicknames, like possums-on-a-half-shell, armored pig, and hoover hog. We refuse to succumb to the notion that any contact with these distant kin to sloths might leave us with leprosy or worse, with badly taxidermized versions of their bony plates pitifully displayed on bars in Texican cantinas. Rather than being repulsive, there is truly something touching about armadillos being asymptomatic carriers of the leprosy-causing bacterium *Mycobacterium leprae*. This affliction also infects the poor and marginalized of our own kind, for whom armadillos offer themselves as a model to epidemiologists who wish to reduce the pathos, pain, and premature mortality caused by that debilitating pathogen. To place them in more lyrical biblical terms, can we imagine that these humble ones—who have for far too long suffered our scorn, sarcasm, and derision—may someday become our actual saviors, dying on the crossroads between laboratory benches, centrifuges, and DNA sequencers so that others may live?

ELEVEN

SONORAN DESERT TOAD

High or Alive and Whole?

Just how did a modest-sized animal that has sat on its haunches, hopped along, and burrowed into the mud for thousands of years without much notice suddenly become a global legend? How did a homely toad gain worldwide recognition in less than twenty years after a "little secret" (or "secretion") leaked out about it?

This is what has recently happened to an old friend of mine, the Sonoran Desert toad, who now goes by the scientific name of *Incilius alvarius*. Its status suddenly changed from being a humble but hefty amphibian—that only appeared above ground with the onset of the desert's summer monsoons—to a superstar on the psychedelics circuit, where tens of thousands of recreational and therapeutic drug users from at least two dozen countries now crave a chance to gain wisdom and healing from this toad.

The inner ear filled with creaking
groans of glands swelling taut.

The wisdom and healing are said to occur simply by inhaling this toad's "God molecule." This enzyme uniquely converts a type of bufotenine found in many other toad species into the distinctive compound 5-MeO-DMT. Also called methylbufotenin, the hallucinogen is five times more potent than street-grade DMT, a controlled substance in the United States.

What's more, it is easily extracted from the toad's exterior glands and can be prepared in several ways for human use or abuse. In the proper settings and dosages, life-changing hallucinations may be generated by this powerful psychedelic substance, but it is otherwise considered a lethal toxin, having been known for centuries for its capacity to kill dogs and native wildlife of the Sonoran Desert in a matter of minutes.

To date, the Sonoran Desert toad is the only vertebrate animal known in the world to produce 5-MeO-DMT, a fact first reported by biochemical pharmacologists in a scientific journal in the late 1960s, just as interest in psychedelic "tripping" exploded on the American scene.

And yet it took two more decades before the "genie got out of the bottle," thanks to a modest pamphlet called "*Bufo alvarius*: The Psychedelic Toad of the Sonoran Desert," published by Albert Most in a short-run printing by Venom Press in Denton, Texas. Now a true cult classic, it has undergone many more printings, with new introductions, and was featured in December 2020 as part of season 3 of the *Vice* docuseries on little-known drugs, *Hamilton's Pharmacopeia*.

This humble piece of ephemera was all that was needed to put the Sonoran Desert toad on the map of thrill-seekers in 1984. Of course, most readers don't associate that particular year with toads, but with a novel in which George Orwell prophesied that society would slump into a totalitarian state in his chilling dystopian novel, *1984*.

Ironically, in a comparable novel written in the same era by Aldous Huxley, *Brave New World*, authorities used an antidepressant and hallucinogenic drug named *soma* to eliminate any residual unhappiness that plagued members of their totalitarian society.

Could the toad-generated DMT hallucinogen and antidepressant be the ticket for helping 21 million Americans gain relief from depressive disorders so they might live happily ever after with one another? Or would a numbed, dumbed-down populace slip into a top-down controlled dystopia thanks to their indulgence in such drugs?

These potent possibilities and fears were not at all on my mind when I first heard about and met the Sonoran Desert toad in my early twenties. I thought they were just one more pretty face in the desert that celebrated the arrival of summer rainfall by holding all-night orgies out in the hinterlands.

At that time in my life, I had just begun fieldwork and guest-teaching in and around Indigenous communities, and I first heard elders relate the arrival of much-needed rains to the appearance of Sonoran Desert toads (then called *Bufo alvarius*). The Tohono O'odham elders I knew were thrilled to hear several kinds of toads arrive with flash floods to congregate and mate in nearby ponds, where they offered symphonic music to anyone who went out to hear them.

Soon after hearing one of those toad concertos, one elder of the desert people took me up to a sacred cave so that she could leave offerings there. Her family had mentioned to her that it once held an ancient toad effigy carved from green stone.

It was one of many cultural expressions—including songs and wood carvings—that they associated with the goodness and sacredness of rains that they knew were essential to their survival in the desert. Although we did not see the toad effigy on that visit, we were touched by the dozens of other offerings placed in a cave high in the mountains "where the rains came from."

To the south of the Tohono O'odham, among the Comcaac in fishing villages on the coast of the Sea of Cortés, there was a similar celebration for the arrival of Sonoran Desert toads with summer rains. Several families I have known for decades still hike down the beach after the first intense rains of the summer to see if floods in the arroyos have carried any of the toads from the inland desert all the way out to the seashore. Their coastal watershed begins twenty to thirty miles inland, where rainfall is more frequent. Because toads are otherwise rare near their villages and only briefly remain frolicking in the tidewater there, it was a special seasonal treat to "greet" the toads in the presence of young children.

But what was it in their minds—*not mine*—that was so delightful about the synchrony of rains, floods, and toads? Were they grateful to see the toads because it meant that sufficient rain had come to reinvigorate the desert plants and wildlife, or were they sure that the toads brought the rains? I have never assumed that any other culture or individual imagines cause-and-effect the same way I do, so this *interrogante* remained an open question in my mind and heart for years.

Happily, Felipe Molina—my old friend and former co-worker from the Marana Yaqui (or Yoemem) community—and his co-author, Richard Felger, finally explained this in beautiful detail: Sonoran Desert toads could not only foreshadow but, in ways, helped initiate the rains that brought vitality to the desert:

> Toads are seen as harbingers of rain. In Pótam, and elsewhere in the Yoem *Bwiara*, if there was a severe drought, the people would have a procession with a toad (*kaureepa*) on a funeral bier. This would take place in the dry season of early summer for the purpose of bringing rain. The toad is decorated with red ribbons and there would be songs and prayers. In the procession, following the toad, people carry a statue of San Isidro, the patron saint of farmers.

The co-appearance of a Sonoran Desert toad called *kaureepa* in Yaqui and the Catholic San Isidro el Labrador is a stunning example of "syncretism," or metaphorical overlap, between certain Indigenous and Spanish Catholic beliefs in the desert borderlands.

San Isidro—who was born to a Mozarabic family in medieval Spain—was not only the saint of farmers, but of well-witchers, irrigators, and "drainsmen" (specialized plumbers for pipes in public works). He is said to have kept water running lavishly out of springs and wells through the community's acequias that carried irrigation water to fields. This saint from Torrelaguna, Spain—like Sonoran Desert toads—blesses fields and ponds with his presence, brings rainwaters to them, and discourages droughts that might otherwise leave poor families thirsty and starving.

Throughout Arizona, Sonora, and New Mexico to this day, devotions and processions for San Isidro are expressions of the hope for plentiful but gentle rains, for the prevention of hailstorms and damaging floods, and for abundant harvests of both wild and cultivated fare.

With all this in my head and heart from my very first days in the desert, I am grateful for Sonoran Desert toads regardless of whether others might see them as potential carriers of the "God molecule."

As for my own interactions with the "keeper and protector of all things wet" in the desert, I first met said toad after agreeing to do some house-sitting for an elderly woman in the Tucson foothills. She threw me her house keys and said nonchalantly,

> You shouldn't have any difficulties dealing with anything inside or outside the house. That is, unless it rains like hell during a monsoon storm that comes in earlier than usual. If that happens, just be sure [to] check the gutters and the swimming pool and any other place where something or someone is likely to get stuck.

Two nights later, I briefly awakened during an unanticipated thunderstorm to a chorus of whistling screeches and moans coming from nearby. I fell asleep and nearly forgot about all the racket.

Most toads, along with a wide range of other animals, have a semitransparent "third eyelid" called a nictitating membrane, which helps protect and moisten their eye without the interruption of vision from a full blink or closure.

But when I woke up at dawn the next morning, I heard similar sounds—perhaps more muted—as well as water being tossed about by someone, or something, splashing and swimming.

When I walked out onto the back patio above the pool, I was surprised to find eighty to a hundred interlopers who had not asked for permission to swim in my friend's private pool.

I couldn't figure out whether the Sonoran Desert toads had emerged from the wet desert soil immediately surrounding the fenced-in pool and patio, or whether they had circumvented the five-foot retaining wall that separated the swimming area from the surrounding desert. A culvert connected them.

Using what little wits I had that early in the morning, I pulled a garbage can over to the area just above the ladder on the shallow side of the pool, then spent over an hour chasing one Sonoran Desert toad after another around the tiled *alberca*. I used a netted filter basket to scoop them out of the water and into the can, which I immediately sealed shut with a lid.

Yes, they were a bit slimy, warty, and meaty compared with other toads in the desert, but they seemed as though they had truly enjoyed a night of "hopping and humping on the wild side." It is also when I first felt their "warm embrace"—technically known as *amplexus*—the reproductive "hug" in which the males clasp females with their front legs to fertilize the mothers' eggs as they are being laid and released. As I grasped the toads to toss them in the can that I would carry away to a still-running wash, they grasped me as well. I am not sure the feeling was mutual, but it moved me to whistle my own little bluegrass tune, "Amplexus Before Breakfast."

With that, I lost my status as an innocent bystander at toad orgies, so from then on, I could never be excused for being a voyeur. I guess you could say that from then on, I had skin in the game.

Interacting with that first cohort of toads gave me my real baptism into life in the desert, alerting me that abundance could suddenly appear out of nowhere in the arid landscape that I had recently chosen as my home. I had never heretofore imagined that I would be swimming buck naked with a squiggle of toads in a luxury pool in the suburbs of Tucson.

By the very next summer, I had been put on the alert list to receive calls at any hour to a SWAT team of herpetologists studying toad orgies. Dennis Cornejo and Clay May had been taking turns running out to a particular cattle tank or charco pond basin to see if enough rain had come in the watershed above it to bring a raft of toads in to begin the orgy. The pond was selected because it held not one, not two, but three different toads that used its waters for reproductive purposes: Hammond's spadefoot, Couch's spadefoot, and the big dudes, Sonoran Desert toads.

In retrospect, I can see why nocturnal mucking around in a muddy reservoir with headlamps on might not be everyone's cup of tea. We'd have to keep our eyes alert for rattlesnakes that had been displaced by the arrival of floodwaters and get into the depths of the pond itself as quickly as possible. Then we would have to capture and quickly identify which toad we grasped and keep a tally of the number of females and males of each species in an exercise aptly called "random sampling."

Of course, the amount of mud covering each toad made this nighttime exercise fraught with uncertainties, and there was more mud at this orgy than there was at the one at Yasgur's Farm near Woodstock, New York, during the summer rains of 1969.

As a botanist on my maiden voyage of sailing into a sea of toads, I was rather inept at this sorting, compared with my five more herpetologically seasoned friends, who seemed to be able to distinguish the species from one another in less time than it would take me to sing a bar of "Froggie Went a-Courtin.'"

These toads were drenched up to their eyes in mud, so that the diagnostic traits used to distinguish one taxon from the next in illustrious field guides were obscured, such that much of the prepping I had undertaken prior to arriving at the pond went down the proverbial drain. I could not tell which spadefoot toads I grabbed and pulled up into the beam of the headlamp had the sickle-shaped spade on their hind foot nuptial pad that was characteristic of *Scaphiopus*, and which had the less angular and roundish spade diagnostic of *Spea*.

As a sleepy-headed novice, I was also having a hard time seeing whether the toad in my hand had eyes with the vertical pupils of spadefoots, or eyes with the horizontal pupils of the puffier Sonoran Desert toads of the genus *Incilius*.

To make matters worse, all the toads were so hyped up and horny that they were no longer mating in twos but were aggregating in long chains—linear "hook-ups" of multiple individuals—that stretched out like an accordion when I tried to lift them up out of the waters.

How could I discern the relative abundance of the three different toads when the males showed no concern for whether their nuptial pads were grasping females of their own species or another? And yet my colleagues seemed to be able to distinguish one species from another, even though I was failing miserably at that same task. I was flummoxed for a while, but then, rather suddenly, I came to my senses. As any proficient naturalist learns to do, we *all* must come to our senses.

The visual diagnostics in the field guide were simply not the sole cues to use in such a setting. To solve this riddle of identity and to record the proper ratio of the three kinds of toads that had come to celebrate together that night, I needed to shift my synesthetic balance. I had to *listen* and smell.

And when I did, what I heard was that some of the toads were letting loose with cries that reminded me of the bleating of Churro sheep, while the Hammond's spadefoots nearby sounded out a short metallic trill that was like the scraping of a ratchet. In contrast, the Sonoran Desert toads burst into song with a low-pitched screech a bit like a ferry boat whistle.

"Hey compadres!" I yelled out to Dennis and Paul, my closest friends on the crew, "Which of the three toad species sings 'Whaah! Whaah! Whaaaaah!' like a lamb looking for its mother?"

"That's the Couch's spadefoot: 'Whaah! Whaah! Whaaaaah!'" Dennis clarified. I realized that was in fact the sound being made by the very toad that was clinging to my gloved hand as if he was ready to mate with it. I had to *sniff* out the peculiar fragrances before me. And when I did, I was able to ask my friends a question that I could not have articulated before that wondrous night:

"And which one has that thick, nutty fragrance reminiscent of roasted peanuts?"

"Well . . . some say both spadefoots do," one friend replied.

Another offered, "I pick up that nutty scent more from Couch's spadefoot, the midsized one. For Hammond's spadefoot, I perceive a hint of garlic, but not everyone agrees with me. It's like the dilemma with those who think ponderosa pines all smell like butterscotch, versus those who pick up notes of vanilla in some ponderosas more than others."

"And what about the big dude, *sapo grande*?" I asked. "You know, he looks all shiny and sweaty like those shellacked toads on sale as nicknacks in Nogales—the ones all dressed up in slick mariachi regalia playing trumpets, violins, and stand-up basses . . . so if you sniff one of the Sonoran Desert toads up close, does he have a different fragrance?"

One of the other crew members wagged his finger at me.

"I don't recommend that you do *any* sniffing or licking of those big, fat Sonoran Desert toads. They secrete a milky ooze from the glands on their skin that is loaded with bufo-toxins that evolved as a chemical defense against desert predators . . . it may either get you high or make you die."

It sounded as though my advisor had some personal experience regarding that binary set of options. He was obviously concerned for my welfare, but he also needed the entire crew to hang in there to help him gain precise toad sex ratio tallies that night.

That was all for the better, for it gave me enough time to contemplate how becoming a naturalist does not just happen through *eye-to-brain* cognitive processes; it also comes through the exercise of all of our senses: *smell*, *touch*, *taste*, *sight*, and *sound*. And when all five senses play a role in our field practice, it seems that our *hearts* and *souls* get engaged as well.

And by becoming more attentive through all our senses, we become more quintessentially human, for those are the very vehicles that made us more responsive to particular opportunities in our pluriverse, sending us on the evolutionary trajectory we have taken up until this most recent stitch in time.

But what I learned at the pond had a lasting effect on me: the aquatic creatures in the desert had to respond immediately to a sudden pulse of fresh water, for a reservoir could dry up again in less than two weeks, sometimes in just ten days. Toads and other aquatic creatures had to adapt to this pulse-and-pause economy, rapidly moving through all stages of metamorphosis from egg to adult in a matter of days, not weeks or months. The slower to respond would become toads out of luck. So they swam into the orgy and reveled in it while it lasted.

Ten years later, around 1990, flash floods from another summer thunderstorm appeared to be moving right toward me. The sky was purple, the wind had kicked up dust, and a sprinkle of light rain had suddenly begun to spray down on the thirsty desert vegetation. I must have looked surprised as I listened to a report informing me that all roads out of the park—and over to the Visitor's Center—had been closed due to flash floods and walls of mud. Soon my driveway and road in front of the house were still covered with a two-inch-thick sheen of sheet flow. I had Teva sandals on, so the water depth didn't matter much. As I walked across the road toward the wash, I could not only hear the surge of spadefoot voices, but I could also catch whiffs of roasted peanuts wafting through the air.

When I reached the banks of the usually dry arroyos, I could see dozens of heads of spadefoots bobbing by, along with leaves, twigs, froth, dirty foam, flotsam, and jetsam. The water depth was at least three feet—maybe five, at most—but not enough to drown any swimmers. I realized that a congregation of desert toads would provide great choir music for the next couple of hours. I did not need to change clothes or shoes, so I ran to the garage to get an old inner tube that was still inflated. Within a couple of minutes, I had plunged into the flooded arroyo with the tube and was moving along at about three miles an hour, using my feet to bounce off the banks, or boulders, or tree trunks whenever needed.

It was not hard to navigate past the hazards in most cases, so I could devote most of my attention to the toads bobbing along beside me. Sometimes it takes a fluke encounter with another species—one where we can meet it on its own terms, at its own speed—to remind us just how enchanted the world can be.

I was basically doing what the Couch's spadefoots and Sonoran Desert toads were doing—sailing along on the frothy waves of floodwaters while storm clouds, lightning, and rainbows flashed above me in an equally turbulent sky. The sound of rushing water saturated my ears. The smell of roasted peanuts overwhelmed my nose—no hint of garlic was evident in this wash.

We all moved along slowly, peaceably, the two toad species and me, for there was no real race with the toads to get to the borrow pit before anyone else. But once the floods fanned out in the shallow gravel quarry of the borrow pit, the soundscape shifted dramatically. It was as if I had a front-row seat to the Vienna Boys' Choir of spadefoots. There were so many voices rising and resonating off the stony borrow-pit banks that it felt as though I had been invited to a private performance by the world's best throat singers. And I had been. I was ecstatic.

There is no other word to describe the thrill of being among such mud-mottled singers, such dogged swimmers, such hedonistic mates on their finest day of the year. So much mud. So much music. So much unabashed joy, even though I had not inhaled the God molecule.

I struggled to remember four stunning sentences from the O'odham creation narrative that my desert anthropology teacher Bernard "Bunny" Fontana used to recite to us:

"Long ago, they say, when the earth was not yet finished, darkness lay upon the water. The turbulent, muddy water and the dark night air rubbed against each other. And the sound they made was like the sound at the edge of a pond. And there, where the moistening rain, the flood waters, the dark skies and the turbulent air came together, the spirit rose up like a wind, and a child was born."

There is a story among the Yaqui that is similar in some respects to the O'odham creation narrative, but different in many others. It is not about a human baby being born, but about Bobok the toad. This abbreviated version certainly does not do full justice to Yoemem storytelling but offers a hint of their regard for toads.

Because their lagoons and ponds had nearly dried up, Bobok the toad had promised the Yaqui council that he would visit the sky spirit to ensure that the rains would come again. He was given the wings of a bat so that he could fly along with the storm front, dancing along in the rainstorm and singing. When he stopped singing, the rain stopped, but when he began again, the rains knew that he was still alive, so they moistened the Yaqui lands as Bobok and the rains arrived together.

As folklorist Ruth Giddings recorded the story, "Since that time, the toads have multiplied and whenever they sing, the rain comes looking for the toads to bless the earth with water."

However rudimentary these translations and adaptations from the O'odham and Yaqui languages may be, they speak to the *inherent* value of the toad—an aquatic creature—as integral to the life of the desert, not apart from it. And for many, the intrinsic value of Sonoran Desert toads is not reduced to that one molecule within them—the so-called God molecule. The toad in its entirety matters more than any chemical compound extracted from it by laboratory reductionists or by drug cartels.

We now live in an era when Sonoran Desert toad populations are being reduced, diminished, and endangered in their habitats on both sides of the U.S.-Mexico border. They were being clandestinely captured in several desert national parks until law enforcers stepped up their level of vigilance during the monsoon season. With the extended droughts that have come with climate change, fewer rain-fed ponds mean fewer toads, which results in higher prices, furtive poaching, and more toads at risk. I know of one case of an Indigenous toad collector being kidnapped by a drug cartel, which forced him to reveal the locations of his toad gathering grounds.

Our society must eventually ask whether the quest for the God molecule for a seven-minute high is worth the decimation of a toad species unlike any other. It seems to me that in valuing its God molecule more than the toad in its entirety, we can't see the forest for the trees.

MEXICAN GRAY WOLF

When I was in my twenties, an elderly Tohono O'odham friend stopped his old pickup truck below the Kitt Peak National Observatory at the place where he had seen one of the last wild-born gray wolves that had come into his homeland. The sighting must have occurred sometime after World War II, when bounty hunters were still authorized to kill any wolf consuming cattle—a practice that continued in Arizona until 1973. From a distance, he thought the bounty hunter's flatbed carried a coyote, but when he arrived to stand next to the hunter's truck, the canid covered the entire surface of the flatbed. It must have reminded him of a strange man with shamanistic leanings from his community, who would disappear for days at a time, and live as a wolf might live, then return to his wife, exhausted by his journey. I knew another Indigenous hunter, still alive, who witnessed wolves on the desert edge of Laguna de la Cruz, the river mouth of the Río Sonora, where it once dumped into the Sea of Cortés. He was young then, but his tribal elders, who also witnessed the wolf, guessed that it was chasing the rare Sonoran pronghorn (antelope) more than a hundred miles south of where they are still seen today. I have worked for a spell on one of Ted Turner's ranches in New Mexico, where I could hear the wolves howling in the pack he uses for reintroductions back onto the larger landscape around the Sky Islands. And I have seen reintroduced ones on a friend's farm in Shoshone, Idaho, but I never expected to hear a wild-born wolf in Arizona. Then one night in 2011, when I was house-sitting for a friend in a deep canyon off Sonoita Creek, a blood-curdling cry rose into the air on a full moon night. Our two Rottweilers—who usually remained nonplussed whenever they heard coyote howls—suddenly began to whimper, then slunk under the bed where my wife and I were sitting up, puzzled by what we had heard. Had wolves come back on their own volition into the mountain ranges of south-central Arizona, or is our desire to let them be at home on their own again in the wilds so strong that all four of us—two dogs and two humans—had the same aural hallucination of their return?

ONZA

There is something about cats—big, toothy, predatory ones—that gets under our skin but also enters our psyche before there is much conscious notice. While in my twenties, I first read about the *onza* in Father Ignaz Pfefferkorn's *Sonora: A Description of the Province,* written in 1760. In his chapter dedicated to the animal kingdom represented in that desert province, the Padre's *onza* description followed right after his comments on what we call a cougar: "The *onza* is in shape [much like the wild cat just described]; however it has a longer body, which is noticeably thinner and narrower, especially toward the rump. Its feet are shorter, its chest, however, much broader . . . It is not as timid as the cougar and he who ventures to attack it must be well on his guard." Another Jesuit, Johann Baegert, wrote from Baja that "an *onza* dared to invade my neighbor's mission when I was visiting, and attacked a fourteen-year-old boy in broad daylight . . . And killed the strongest and most respected soldier." There can be no doubt that these well-educated natural historians and chroniclers were discussing a feline that they regarded as distinct from and equal to a mountain lion, and not an imaginary one. Another

decade in my life passed before I heard about the *onza* firsthand from mestizo and Guarijio farmers and ranchers in the Sierra Madre, just north and east of Álamos, Sonora. On a mule trip with two friends from Arizona, every family we stayed with had their own story of the *onza* or the livestock it had killed, and they were rather matter-of-fact in their descriptions about this seldom-seen cat. On the same trip, I first met the rancher, Criollo cattle buyer, and novelist, J. P. S. Brown, up at a ranch on the Continental Divide close to the Sonora-Chihuahua border. Later on, when I got to know Joe as my neighbor in Patagonia, Arizona, he confirmed he had heard from campesinos many stories of the *onza* that distinguished it from the predatory *tigre*—the *yoco* or jaguar—and it was of a reddish-brown color like immature mountain lions, but longer and leaner than most mountain lions or jaguars. In *The Forests of the Night,* Brown conceded that the identity of *onza* in the barrancas was problematic at best: "He was called *onza*. The *onza* is a large feline of the Sierra that is said to be a cross between the cougar and the jaguar, or the mutation of a lion, or a mythical beast." Many other wildlife aficionados have tried to resolve the issue. One was a colleague of mine in the early 1980s, Richard Greenwell, who founded the field of cryptozoology and had a desk in the Office of Arid Lands Studies in Tucson, around the corner from my own. He insisted that field biologists should apply their full range of skills and technologies to confirm or deny the continuing presence of cryptids—living beings that remain hidden or scientifically undocumented, but that deserve to be the subjects of investigation. I remember discussing the *onza* with him over coffee one day around 1984. He chuckled when I brought up the questionable status of the *onza* among academic biologists, as well as the veracity of Mexican wildlife hunters' regard for it. And then he quipped, "As far as I can see, the *onza* should be *fair game* . . . for some interesting explorations." Around 1995, Richard and I attended a conservation biology conference where geneticists reported the results of DNA analysis of a wild cat carcass purported to be an *onza*. It had been shot in January 1986 by rancher Andrés Rodríguez

Murillo in Sinaloa. Richard was sad to learn that this animal's genes were the same as those of mountain lions. But I was happy to see that there is more to the story than mitochondrial DNA. At one level, campesinos do not much care whether a genomics lab determines that one wild cat's DNA is the same or different, because these traditional carriers of age-old stories of the *onza* may not be technically describing a fierce cat hidden in a barranca, as much as one looming large in their psyche. Big cats have been steadily portrayed in the art of American cultures for upward of three thousand years, exemplifying what eco-philosopher Julie Hawkins has called *The Folklore of Awe,* in which human cultures over millennia have created representations of strange creatures and phenomena as the "other." Will these "wild cats" continue to roam in our corpus of songs and stories forever? Isn't it likely that we will need them to remind us that rational minds are still not in full control of the world within and around us?

TWELVE

BOOJUMS

Animated, Sacred Creatures

From the first time I met a towering, thick-torso, prickly-armed boojum around 1971, I wanted to learn all I could from them and about them from both scientists and Indigenous residents who are their neighbors. This thirst was so great that I once endured two weeks in the desert with eight heat-tolerant friends studying their pollination ecology as ground temperatures rose over 110 degrees Fahrenheit. That same year, I guided a dozen Comcaac Indigenous youth to see this sacred being in the Sierra Bacha on the coast of Sonora, where an elder told them the origin story of this bizarre elder.

As I have gotten older—it is indeed difficult to get younger!—I am more and more bemused by how Western science and Indigenous knowledge carried in oral histories tell us completely different things about the creatures in this world. When I was starting out as

New bodies twist shut after
floodwaters subside.

an ethnobiology fieldworker, I naïvely wished that the two ways of knowing would fall into perfect alignment.

That would "prove" that the traditional knowledge of desert dwellers was both precise and parsimonious with that of academic scientists, which is a conceit that I now find to be ethnocentric and rather silly in most cases. Even the argument that Indigenous knowledge is more "accurate" or explanatory than Western scientific findings can be ethnocentric as well. These two ways of knowing are often done for very different reasons, with very different cosmologies, ethics, timelines, and tools or technologies.

As Samuel Clemens is said to have once quipped, "Never the twain shall meet!" It is entirely okay that different ways of knowing the natural world inform and enrich us *without* telling us the same stories about who our plant and animal neighbors are. Their narratives are not only divergent but sometimes appear paradoxical or contradictory when compared with one another. That alone might awaken some of us to possibilities that we might not have otherwise recognized, which is worth the ticket price for being alive, as far as I am concerned.

Let me offer an outrageous example of the incongruous and antithetical ways that Western scientists and Indigenous cosmologists regard the same organism. Its folk name in English is the boojum; in Spanish, the *cirio* (a thick candle with a waxy surface); and in the Linnean Latin lingo of academic scientists, *Fouquieria columnaris*.

Let us start with the latter to reveal how different ways of knowing regard the same desert icon—a species with a pale, towering trunk that reaches as high as seventy feet off the ground, that looks like an upside-down carrot given too much fertilizer, emanating the sweet fragrance of honey.

Scientists simply see it as one more species akin to the sprangly ocotillos that look like the first television antennae installed in living rooms in the 1950s. It was first described in a scientific publication in 1860 as a distinctive (monotypic) species in a new genus of plants named *Idria*. This plant was found growing over a wide range of Baja California, most notably in a nearly rainless area near Cataviña, where it grows so densely that it is now called the Boojum Forest.

Its flowers and vegetative structures were later found to resemble two ocotillo species in central Mexico more than those that grew with it in the Sonoran Desert, so it was lumped into the *Fouquieria* genus with ten other kin, which is the sole group that comprises the family known as the Fouquieriaceae. Western academic scientists claim that this group of plants has an ancient origin, emerging as a distinctive family around 100 million years ago. Geologists recently estimated that the Baja California peninsula "rifted away" from mainland Mexico about 6 million years ago, and many botanists believed that is when *Fouquieria columnaris* began to diverge from other ocotillos and take its peculiar shape as a treelike succulent with spiky branches. If needed, it can take up water accumulated by its roots and store it in its trunk for many months if not years.

For decades, botanists believed that this species was an "endemic," found only on the Baja California peninsula, but they later learned that it was also found on the fog-shrouded summit of Isla Ángel de la Guarda in the Sea of Cortés, and across the sea on the Mexican mainland in just one mountain range, the Sierra Bacha.

To explain how these three isolated boojum populations came into being, some Mexican botanists posited that the Comcaac, or their Indigenous ancestors, consciously transplanted a few boojums, which then became established and multiplied on their own accord.

The Comcaac of Sonora reject that they themselves moved the plants to these two isolated places for several reasons, all of which seem outrageous to scientists.

First off, the Comcaac do not put the being they call Cototaj in the same category as ocotillos or other trees; they claim it is a gigantic kind of sentient being—like massive manta rays, a few columnar

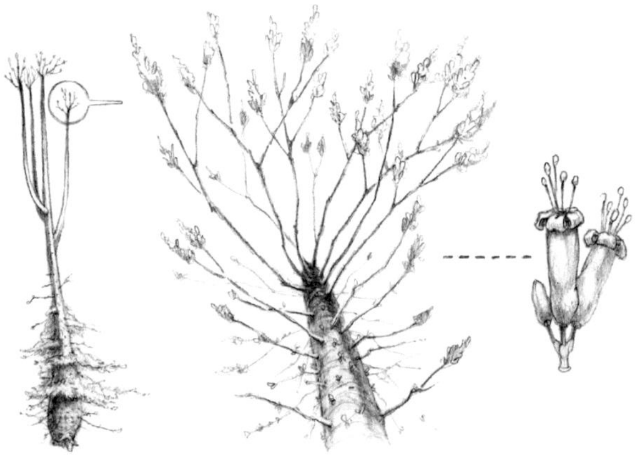

"Its flowers and vegetative structures were later found to resemble two ocotillo species in central Mexico more than those that grew with it in the Sonoran Desert, so it was lumped into the Fouquieria genus with ten other kin."

cacti, and leatherback sea turtles—that are aligned with humans. In fact, they sense that boojums have some affinities that characterize mobile animals more than sessile plants. They say that boojums "ran" over from Baja California while escaping an ancient flood that filled a basin, the one we now call the Sea of Cortés! To Comcaac elders, this being is placed in a group of "sacred" or "supernatural" beings that share ancestry with humans more than with most desert or sea plants and animals.

The ancestors they shared with the Comcaac were said to be "giants" from the Baja California peninsula, which is a curious contention, given that the fish-and-meat-eating Indigenes of Baja California were, in fact, much taller than the corn-and-bean-eating farmers on mainland Mexico today. For the Comcaac to claim that they were descended from "sacred giants" living in a nonagricultural region remote from most of Mexico carries some plausibility.

Regarding the Comcaac kinship with Cototaj, we need not go back in time 6 million or 100 million years, as the paleobotanists do. Instead, we need to stretch our imaginations to envision a primordial moment in time when plants, animals, and peoples readily communicated with one another, and on occasion, changed forms.

If we can imagine the spiritual power of gigantic beings was sufficient to morph them into other forms during that bygone time, then the origin narrative that the late Adolfo Burgos told his grandchildren, nieces, and nephews in the Sierra Bacha is dramatically explanatory:

> In those times, what you see up on the hilly slopes were people, giant people named the Cototaj. They were once people who [ran across from Baja California in a dry basin] and were trying to climb high up to the tops of the hills when [the Great Flood] happened, filling the low-lying areas with water. They were climbing because they were terrified of the tide that was rising. In those times, tidal waves would come now and then to try to terminate the world, to finish off its people. The Cototaj were so scared that they were trying to escape their doom. The floodwaters reached the slowest of them and swallowed them up.
>
> But the ones that reached the lower slopes above the basin presumed they had escaped without harm or death and stopped running. Then the highest reach of the tides splashed its sea foam against their heels, and the touch of the flood changed them from giant people into the giant forms you see on the slopes above you.
>
> So we can say they remain sacred people today, and we have a taboo against breaking even the slightest branch or spike off their bodies. They are our ancestors, which is to say, each is one of us, and should not be harmed by our actions.

I was reeling as I listened to Adolfo's narrative, watching older women weep, holding the hands of small children who trembled with the power of that ancient story. The Comcaac did not *bring* boojums from Baja California, because the sacred boojums were *them*.

Even in Spanish, there is a sense of the sacred embedded in the folk name that Sonorans use for these plants: *cirios*. The translation of *cirio* as a fat, waxy candle or candelabra doesn't quite reflect the spiritual dimensions of this term. For Catholics, the cirio is the paschal candle at Easter time that keeps the light of Jesus burning brightly after his terrible crucifixion, casting away the darkness. When folk Catholics face tragedies in Sonora, *cirios* are lit to remind them that Jesus came as a light in the desert, to cast away crisis, chaos, or sickness by reaffirming the Creator's presence among his faithful.

The folk name for this being in English is stranger still, coming from the Lewis Carroll poem *The Hunting of the Snark* when the British-born naturalist and widower Godfrey Sykes took his two young sons on a long expedition into the Sonoran Desert. I once heard Godfrey's son, Glenton, tell how fond his father was of reading Lewis Carroll poems to him and his brother. Glenton and Gilbert grew up reciting some of those poems, so the passages were familiar to them. When they were out camping together in 1922, Godfrey looked out into the desert through his telescope and exclaimed, "Ho! Ho! Definitely a boojum!" It tickled the boys to no end.

They quickly recited a reference to an earlier expedition that Lewis Carroll had referred to at the end of his 1876 poem about the slippery sighting of a snark:

> "It's a snark!" was the sound that first came to their ears,
> And it seemed almost too good to be true.
> Then followed a torrent of laughter and cheers:
> Then the ominous words "It's a Boo-"

Then silence. Some fancied they heard in the air
A weary and wandering sigh
That sounded like "-jum!" but the others declare
It was only a breeze that went by . . .

In the midst of the word he was trying to say
In the midst of his laughter and glee,
He had softly and suddenly vanished away—
For the Snark *was* a Boojum, you see."

As I can personally attest, anyone who later heard Godfrey's son Glenton recount that naming was so charmed and humored by his storytelling acumen that the name *boojum* spread like wildfire by word of mouth from one naturalist or botanist to another. It was used in plant manuals and on plaques in botanical gardens in Arizona and California, where millions of tourists have fallen into rapture over this quirky, carrot-like monstrosity.

More than six decades after Godfrey Sykes had thrilled his sons with the sighting of the boojum that gave them their English name, I took some junior high kids to see boojums in central Baja California. We stopped in the legendary Boojum Forest near Cataviña to walk among these elders of the desert. I repeated Godfrey's exclamation to them as we wandered around in the dense forest of these giants, some of them towering above us, while others were bent, with their "heads" touching the ground. One of the young girls smiled as I told her the story of how boojums got their name, then she silently crawled under one of the plants that formed a perfect arch over her head. She then lay down, belly up, on the ground

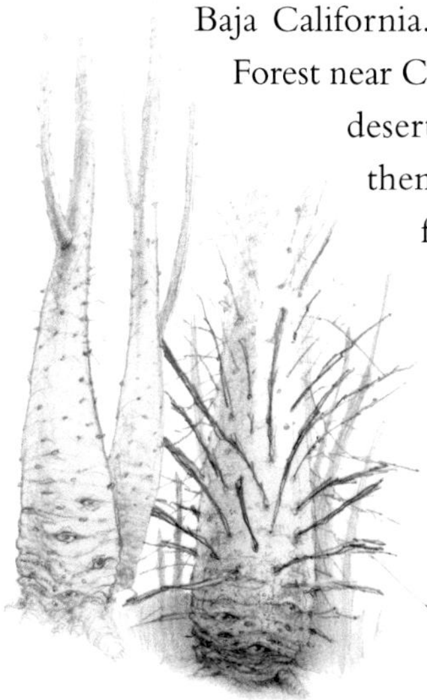

below the arching boojum, and raised herself in a backbend that perfectly reflected the curvature of the thick trunk above her.

I must have moaned with delight, with the irony of it all: she, too, was a human becoming a boojum, much like the Comcaac ancestors may have done centuries before us.

I have only recently become aware that the folk term *boojum* has continued to take on new meanings. It can be a bag, backpack, rucksack, satchel, or morral that students use to carry books to school.

It is the nickname of a famous African American baseball player, Jud "Boojum" Wilson, who hit line drives so hard that the peculiar noise they made when hitting an outfield fence was so indescribable that another player blurted out "Boojum!" for none on the team had ever heard anything like it before!

It is a much-loved chain of restaurants featuring Mexican burritos that began in Belfast on Botanic Avenue and has spread as far as Dublin, where a Turbo Boojum now feeds thousands of lovers of pungent, piquant, peppery, turbo-powered foods.

It is the name of an XSSM-A-5 model of the Snark supersonic intercontinental cruise missile designed to carry a W39 thermonuclear warhead, which I hope will someday "softly and suddenly vanish away."

It is a geometric pattern on the surface of a superfluid called *helium-3*, whose motion exemplifies a "vanishing behavior" in low-temperature physics first described in 1976 by physicist and pianist David Mermin.

It is even the name of a garage-punk band from Nova Scotia.

These are all "different ways of knowing" what a boojum is and what it may become in the future. Together they remind us that art and story inform science, and science informs art and story. And they also remind us that boojums do not stay static as plants are thought to be, but remain animated, fleshy, fresh, and untamed.

ACKNOWLEDGMENTS

Both of us are so grateful for the warm reception this project has received from University of Arizona Press staff superstars Kristen Buckles, Kathryn Conrad, Amanda Krause, Leigh McDonald, Abby Mogollon, Mary Reynolds, and Elizabeth Wilder. Like Gary's 1985 book with artist Paul Mirocha, *Gathering the Desert*, we are delighted by the way the Press staff sees this as a truly collaborative effort between an artistic author and a literary author, with each riffing off the other.

FROM ROBERT, THE ARTIST

Thank you, Gary, for reaching out to me to work on this book with you. It's been a pleasure and an honor making art in dialogue with your written words. I'd like to thank Professor Grey Gustafson for access to *Atta* ants, *Eleodes* beetles, *Rothschildia* moths, and *Triops* shrimp in the Arthropod Collection at Northern Arizona University. I should also thank the couple of bugs who posed for photos or croaked in convenient places around my yard. I also thank Northern Arizona University for offering some wiggle room in my teaching contract to work on this book. Professors Ellen McMahon and Dave Christiana of the University of Arizona School of Art: you connected countless dots for me and inspired me throughout two degrees and beyond. Michael Nolan of Pima Community College: you made two-dimensional design truly make sense in a way that sticks with me always. My friend Mary Wolfe has been giving me loads of farm-fresh vegetables, and my drawing hand and eyeballs thank you for the influx of vitamins. I thank my good buddies Christopher Paiva and Joseph Meny for the memories we made crabbing on the Chesapeake, and my good buddy Griffin Marsh for always being there to talk for hours about our ridiculously identical interests. And finally, I am eternally grateful to my parents for providing pencils and paper to such a young seedling, for nudging me away from the television and into the backyard, for taking me on childhood road trips (when I too adopted a jumping bean), and for encouraging me to this day in all of my artistic and biological pursuits.

FROM GARY, THE AUTHOR

Working with Bobby Long has been a true thrill. I am grateful for the moral support from my clan of Laurie Monti, Curt Meine, Jeremy and Jessica Smith, DeJa Walker, Amadeo Rea, Susan Kunz, Derrick Widmark, David Fain, and Ruby the Aussie shepherd dog.

I have felt especially honored and humbled to have been in dialogue over many years with Indigenous scholars and storytellers, including Alberto Mellado Jr., Erika Barnett, Ofelia Zepeda, Vernon Masayesva, Melissa Nelson, Dennis Martinez, Isabel Cristina Murrieta López, Felipe Molina, Robert Valencia, Maria Luisa Estrella, Manuel Monroy, José Luis Blanco, Delores Lewis, José Antonio "Delfino" Magayan, Juan Arguelles, Alfredo Lopez Blanco, Guadalupe Lopez Blanco, Amalia Astorga, Adolfo Burgos, Gabriel Hoeffer, Roberto Camposano, and Danny Lopez, just to name a few. Bless you, your families, and your communities.

I have been informed and inspired over the years by several great desert artists and writers including Paul Mirocha, Bill Singleton, Tom Weiwandt, Big Jim Griffith, J. P. S. Brown, Ben Wilder, Beto Villa, Howard Scott Gentry, Harry Winter, Alberto Burquez Montijo, Ruben Martinez, Enrique La Madrid, Dan Matson, Dave Brown, Wade Sherbrooke, Lee Grismer, W. S. Minckley, Ray Turner, Kathleen Alcalá, Bill Broyles, Richard Felger, Tom VanDevender, Dave Steadman, Michael Branch, Marty Camp, Don Bahr, Ruth Giddings, Dennis Cornejo, Bill Calder, Cathy Moser, Steve Marlett, Alison Deming, and Dean and Lucille Saxton.

Finally, I have been inspired by scholars and artists working on these themes, in multiple regions, including Emily Griffith, who brilliantly works on porphyrin pigments; Kimon de Greef and Beto Villa, who investigate the impacts of Sonoran Desert toad harvesting; Alex Mintzer, who has studied Mexican leaf-cutter ants for over three decades; and the late Richard Greenwell, who introduced me to cryptozoology. I am also grateful to old friends Liz Carlisle and Aubrey Streit Krug, who published another version of the Mexican leaf-cutter essay in an anthology from The Land Institute.

ARTIST STATEMENT

The illustrations in this book were drawn on paper with mechanical pencils, using lead sizes of 0.5 mm and finer. I made them into digital files with a scanner and digitally painted in any color using an old version of Adobe Photoshop and a Wacom tablet. I also wrote their captions. No generative artificial intelligence was used in the making of this artwork or this book as a whole. Instead, we did our best to use our heads and hands to commit stories, told with words and drawn marks, into the warm depths of flat paper.

I aim to inspire curiosity about the intricacies and symbioses of the natural world, and by extension, promote nature conservation. Fueled by biology and protoscience, my artwork amplifies intimate and obscure forms of life, giving underrepresented organisms a louder voice and visualizing their self-worlds or *Umwelten*. I stay inspired through reading and macrophotography, by visiting natural history museums and aquaria, and by tending to my collection of unusual plants. A natural curiosity pushes me along, often to places I didn't expect to be.

No animals were harmed in the making of this book.

FURTHER READING

Alibek, Kenneth, Catherine Lobanova, and Serguei Popov. 2005. "1. History of Anthrax." In *Bioterrorism and Infectious Agents: A New Dilemma for the 21st Century*, edited by I. W. Fong and Ken Alibek. Springer.

Borges, Jorge Luis, and Margarita Guerrero. 2005. *The Book of Imaginary Beings*. Andrew Hurley (tr.), Peter Sís (illus.). Viking Penguin.

Branch, Michael P. 2022. *On the Trail of the Jackalope: How a Legend Captured the World's Imagination and Helped Us Cure Cancer*. Pegasus Books.

Brown, David E., and Neil B. Carmony. 1999. *Gila Monster: Facts and Folklore of America's Aztec Lizard*. University of Utah Press.

Brown, J. P. S. 1992. *The Cinnamon Colt and Other Stories*. Doubleday.

Brown, J. P. S. 2008. *The Forests of the Night*. Iuniverse Inc.

Crump, Marty. 2015. *Eye of Newt and Toe of Frog, Adder's Fork and Lizard's Leg: The Lore and Mythology of Amphibians and Reptiles*. University of Chicago Press.

de Greef, Kimon, 2026. *The Ego Trip: Psychedelic Toads, a Trail of Dreams, and the Guru Who Peddled Transcendence*. Penguin Random House.

Felger, Richard S., and Felipe Sylvester Molina. 2024. *Plants and Animals in the Yoeme World: Ethnoecology of the Yaquis in Sonora and Arizona*. Desert Institute Press.

Felger, Richard S., and Mary Beck Moser. 1985. *People of the Desert and Sea*. University of Arizona Press.

Giddings, Ruth W. 1959. *Yaqui Myths and Legends*. University of Arizona Press.

Griffith, Emily V., Nova Mackentley, Chris M. Neri, Brandon M. Canfield, and Alec R. Lindsay. 2025. "Fluorescent Pigment Concentration Correlated with

Age, Sex, and Size in Long-eared Owl (*Asio otus*) Plumage." *Wilson Journal of Ornithology* 137 (2): 1–11.

Griffith, James S. 1993. *Beliefs and Holy Places: A Spiritual Geography of Pimería Alta.* University of Arizona Press.

Hayes, Joe. 2001. *¡El Cucuy! A Bogeyman Cuento in English and Spanish.* Cinco Punto Press.

Hillman, James, and Margo McLean. 1997. *Dream Animals.* Chronicle Books.

Humphrey, Robert R. 1974. *The Boojum and Its Home.* University of Arizona Press.

Hyde, Lewis. 1998. *Trickster Makes This World: Mischief, Myth, and Art.* Farrar, Straus and Giroux.

Manaster, Jane. 2002. *Horned Lizards: The Book of Horny Toads.* Texas Tech University Press.

Marshall, Robert E. 1961. *The Onza: The Story of the Search for the Mysterious Cat of the Mexican Highlands.* Exposition Press.

Minckley, W. L., and Paul C. Marsh. 2009. *Inland Fishes of the Greater Southwest.* University of Arizona Press.

Most, Albert. 1984. "*Bufo alvarius*: The Psychedelic Toad of the Sonoran Desert." Privately printed, then republished by Venom Press.

Muñoz Ledo, Norma, and Israel Barrón. 2016. *Bestiario de Seres Fantásticos Mexicanos.* Fondo de Cultura Económica.

Murrieta López, Isabel Cristina. 2018. *Leyendas y Relatos de Nácori Chico.* Editorial Mini Libros de Sonora.

Purcell, Rosamond. 1997. *Special Cases: Natural Anomalies and Historical Monsters.* Chronicle Books.

Purcell, Rosamond, and Stephen Jay Gould. 1986. *Illuminations: A Bestiary.* W. W. Norton.

Rea, Amadeo M. 2016. *Once a River: Bird Life and Habitat Changes on the Middle Gila.* University of Arizona Press.

Rea, Amadeo M. 2018. *Folk Mammalogy of the Northern Pimans.* University of Arizona Press.

Sherbrooke, Wade C. 2003. *Introduction to Horned Lizards of North America.* California Natural History Guides No. 64, University of California Press.

Swiderski, Richard M. 2004. *Anthrax: A History.* McFarland.

Villa, Robert A. 2023. "Toad in the Road: Biocultural History and Conservation Challenges of the Sonoran Desert Toad." *Journal of Psychedelic Studies* 7 (S1): 68–79.

Winters, Jr., Harry J. 2012. *O'odham Place Names: Meanings, Origins, and Histories, Arizona and Sonora.* Nighthorses.

ABOUT THE AUTHOR AND ILLUSTRATOR

Gary Paul Nabhan is a Lebanese American desert ecologist who served as the Kellogg Endowed Chair in Southwestern Borderlands Food and Water Security at the University of Arizona. He received his PhD from the University of Arizona in 1983. Nabhan is the cofounder of Native Seeds/SEARCH and the founding director of the Center for Sustainable Environments at Northern Arizona University. He is the author of over thirty books, including the James Beard Award-winning *Agave Spirits: The Past, Present, and Future of Mezcals* (W. W. Norton & Company, 2023), *The Nature of Desert Nature* (University of Arizona Press, 2020), *Ethnobiology for the Future* (University of Arizona Press, 2016), *Arab/American* (University of Arizona Press, 2008), *The Desert Smells Like Rain* (University of Arizona Press, 2002), and *Gathering the Desert* (University of Arizona Press, 1985). Nabhan is the recipient of awards, including a MacArthur Genius Award and a Lannan Literary Fellowship, and is a Takreem Foundation Arab American laureate.

Robert J. Long is an associate teaching professor of visual communication at Northern Arizona University. Bobby earned his MFA in studio art at the University of Arizona in 2013. His visual art, made under the pen name NearsightGraphite, has been published in *Frontiers in Microbiology*, *Manifest Press*, the *Confluencenter for Creative Inquiry*, and *Edible Baja Arizona Magazine*, among others. His award-winning work has been shown in juried gallery exhibitions in the United States and abroad since 2008. His art installations include *Undersea Discovery* (2023–present) and *Wild World of Bugs* (2021–present) in the Flandrau Science Center & Planetarium at the University of Arizona. In 2013, he became Arizona's first finalist in the internationally juried Adobe Design Achievement Awards.